THE POINT OF THE GUN

The Definitive Straight-Shooting Guide to
Choosing Firearms for Self Defense.

BRUCE OWEN AND DOUG NICKLE

Written by Doug Nickle

BALBOA PRESS
A DIVISION OF HAY HOUSE

Copyright © 2017 Bruce Owen and Doug Nickle.

All rights reserved. No part of this book may be used or reproduced by any means, graphic, electronic, or mechanical, including photocopying, recording, taping or by any information storage retrieval system without the written permission of the author except in the case of brief quotations embodied in critical articles and reviews.

Balboa Press books may be ordered through booksellers or by contacting:

Balboa Press
A Division of Hay House
1663 Liberty Drive
Bloomington, IN 47403
www.balboapress.com
1 (877) 407-4847

Because of the dynamic nature of the Internet, any web addresses or links contained in this book may have changed since publication and may no longer be valid. The views expressed in this work are solely those of the author and do not necessarily reflect the views of the publisher, and the publisher hereby disclaims any responsibility for them.

The information, ideas, and suggestions in this book are not intended to render legal advice. Before following any suggestions contained in this book, you should consult your personal attorney. Neither the author nor the publisher shall be liable or responsible for any loss or damage allegedly arising as a consequence of your use or application of any information or suggestions in this book.

Any people depicted in stock imagery provided by Thinkstock are models, and such images are being used for illustrative purposes only.
Certain stock imagery © Thinkstock.

Print information available on the last page.

ISBN: 978-1-5043-9045-3 (sc)
ISBN: 978-1-5043-9044-6 (hc)
ISBN: 978-1-5043-9046-0 (e)

Library of Congress Control Number: 2017915970

Balboa Press rev. date: 12/04/2017

ACKNOWLEDGEMENTS

I would like to offer special thanks to Michael Sattinger and Eric Grossman who believed in the concept of the Hub and made it happen; to all the employees and customers of the Hub who became my friends… especially Steve, Howard, Frank and Mike; to Steve and Mindy, two of my first and favorite students; and Rob Hephner, aka Birdman, the brains behind the podcasts. But, I owe the most to Doug Nickle who in writing this book with me made a dream become a reality. For over a year we talked, shot and "lived" guns so we could simplify a profoundly important subject to share the information with friends and soon-to-be friends.

Finally, to my brother Rod for all his support when we first started on this journey and my sister Cheryl who's idea it was for me to write a book. And last, but not least to Kathy and Vanessa…Thank you for putting up with me and helping me get through this process. I owe you!

Bruce Owen

I'd like to thank Bruce Owen for sharing his comprehensive knowledge of firearms with me. We spent the better part of 3 years exploring the most practical aspects of owning firearms for self defense and developed a minimalist, forthright philosophy that answers the question- "What is *the point* of a firearm to be used for personal protection?" We enjoy all aspects of firearms, including shooting sports, competition, hunting etc… but we narrowed the scope of this book to focus on one of the most fundamental reasons for owning a gun- to protect ourselves and those we love.

Thank you to my wife Vanessa and mother-in-law Kathy, for listening in mild amusement as Bruce and I worked through this process. Finally, thank you to my toddler Annabelle who worked right beside me in my office, tapping away on her "puter" (which looks remarkably similar to my desk calculator!).

Doug Nickle

CONTENTS

Chapter 1:   The Point of the Gun 1
Chapter 2:   The Revolver 9
Chapter 3:   Semi-automatic handguns...18
Chapter 4:   Comparing Revolvers and Semi-autos for EDC 27
Chapter 5:   Ammunition basics..41
Chapter 6:   Home Defense Firearms-Shotguns................................49
Chapter 7:   Home Defense: Carbines 59
Chapter 8:   Holsters and other methods of carry for handguns........69
Chapter 9:   Physical Considerations and Recommended Exercises......81
Chapter 10: Recommendations 87
Chapter 11: Case Studies 91
Chapter 12: Additional Resources 98

PREFACE

There are many books about firearms on the market, including authoritative works that discuss guns and their application for self defense. Many focus on the legal ramifications of firearm ownership and deliberate over the role of the 2nd Amendment in modern society.

As more citizens make the decision to purchase their first firearm, and longtime gun owners reevaluate their personal defense strategy, we recognize the need for a straightforward book that will arm law abiding citizens with the information they need when selecting a handgun, shotgun or rifle for self defense.

Consequently, The Point of the Gun was conceived and written to provide both new and experienced gun owners with a no-nonsense guide to choosing the appropriate firearm based on their personal needs and abilities.

Firearms are tools; each are designed for specific tasks, and responsible gun owners are obligated to understand the basic mechanical functionality, safe operation and maintenance of their guns and they must train themselves to be proficient in their use.

We "shoot you straight," providing the fundamental considerations and explanations about defensive firearms so you can decide for yourself what will work best for you. We demystify the subject of firearm ownership and hope to enhance your confidence with the guns you use to protect yourself and your loved ones.

Thank you for reading and sharing this information!

INTRODUCTION

In America's increasingly polarized political environment, our constitutional right to bear arms is under institutional assault. Anti-gun politicians are emboldened by a sensationalist, ratings-driven media that dishonestly misrepresents the facts of most shooting-related incidents, drawing the most extreme and illogical conclusions. Consequently, the 2nd Amendment is now treated as the least of all amendments by those who oppose our individual right to bear arms. Anti-gunners believe the 2nd Amendment is open for interpretation and revision to better fit *their* worldview.

Fortunately, this aggressive multi-front attack on American gun owners is increasingly countered by a newly awakened citizenry. Gun owners know what is at stake, and they've taken up the fight against the anti-gun cabal that is pushing for citizen disarmament. Even citizens who have long been ambivalent or overtly against guns in general are swarming to their local gun shops to buy their first firearms.

Individual gun ownership is a constitutionally protected right, just like freedom of speech. The Second Amendment should unquestionably secure the right to bear arms for law abiding American citizens. So why the recent surge in gun purchases? Just as every tragic gun-related crime emboldens the anti-gunners, such feverish inertia also drives gun owners to their local gun shops, reasonably fearful that legislation might soon prevent them from acquiring tools to protect themselves.

But it goes beyond fear; it's also respect for and defense of the provisions of the United States Constitution. "It shall not be infringed."

We live in a progressively dangerous world. Civilization is marred globally by violent crime and a frightful increase in unconventional acts and methods of terrorism. Many citizens realize that if a violent criminal act is perpetrated on them, they *must be their own first responder.* It is their *right and responsibility* to protect themselves and their loved ones, *before* help arrives. Indeed, a civilized society owes this to itself.

Anti-gunners are all too often a hypocritical bunch. Some well-meaning "antis" can be forgiven for their genuine desire that guns needn't exist in a civilized society. After all, no sane person wants violence of any sort in our daily lives. The problem is, we don't live in that type of civilized Utopian society.

Violence and criminal behavior are facts of life- in our country and in every other country on earth- since the dawn of human existence. Therefore, the anti-gun argument promoting citizen disarmament collapses on itself; the gun laws designed to make gun ownership difficult or impossible only affect *law abiding* citizens. Criminals don't adhere to laws (hence, *criminal*) and bad guys will always gain access to guns and weapons. Therefore, legislatively disarming law abiding citizens creates the environment for their potential victimization.

Many of America's elected leaders and many people in the media are willfully ignorant of such common sense, perhaps even more so of the illegality of attempts to rescind *rights* explicitly *protected* in the United States Constitution and Bill of Rights. Such elected officials stand *behind* the Constitution when politically expedient, yet trample on it given the chance that it will expand power over the people they are sworn to govern. *Thus are the seeds of tyranny sown.*

Since our Republic is governed *of the people, by the people, and for the people*, it is incumbent upon **We the People** to be vigilant in determining who we elect to any political office. **As voters,** we must impose term limits as necessary, in *every election*. Officials who fail to defend the protections provided in the Constitution must be voted out of office. *That's how we can impose term limits*, and we don't need a law to enforce them. **It is that simple**. Yet as evidenced by the general decline in voter turnout over the past 20 years, Americans have effectively abdicated our responsibility for our fellow citizens we elect. By not voting, we elect by *omission- which is still* effectively a mandate for those elected.

The 2nd Amendment is the foundation upon which all others exist. It is now time to exert our collective influence and power by electing policymakers who uphold *all* amendments, **especially the 2nd**.

We have the *inviolable right* to self preservation and this right extends unequivocally to the protection of our loved ones. **No individual or legislative body** may reverse this right. Any organized, governmental or institutional effort to the contrary that would put us at the mercy of criminals and terrorists must be met with an aggressive and legal counter offensive.

Tyranny lurks when citizen apathy plods along unabated. The Second Amendment is as relevant today as it was when ratified in the Bill of Rights in the years following America's war for independence. If, by our careless attention to our rights, we allow our elected and appointed leaders to usurp more of them, *they will assuredly do so*. It is our *duty* as citizens to prevent this from happening. Stand up and be counted in defense of the 2nd Amendment. Vote for fellow citizens who will protect your right to keep and bear arms.

The concerted effort to disarm our populace provides fresh significance to the oath that demands defense of the Constitution against all enemies, foreign *and domestic*.

Doug Nickle
September 2017

CHAPTER 1

THE POINT OF THE GUN

First time gun buyers are surging in numbers in the United States as individual citizens take advantage of their Constitutional right *to keep and bear arms*. The increase in the number of new gun owners is attributed to a handful of factors, such as recent terror attacks perpetrated by individuals or small groups of religiously radicalized men and women. While crimes involving firearms have gone down, an overall increase in violent crime[1] has prompted many citizens to become their own first responders. Consequently, new gun owners have made the wise and courageous decision to arm and protect themselves and their loved ones.

Fortunately, it's not just first time buyers purchasing new guns; many long time gun owners see ominous writing on the political wall. They are apprehensive of legislative efforts that would expropriate their natural and 2nd Amendment rights.

If you are reading this firearm self defense primer, you have made the decision to arm yourself for personal and home defense and you

---

[1] https://www.fbi.gov/news/stories/latest-crime-statistics-released

want practical guidance on just which gun to choose. You are ready to buy a gun for *everyday carry (**EDC**)* and you want to learn how to use it correctly, safely, and responsibly.

Where do you start? How do you sift through the volumes of information and opinions on guns and calibers to make the right decision for you personally? Guns are not one-size-fit-all and choosing the right one for you is a decision that demands careful consideration.

How this book will help you

If you want a gun for self defense, or if you simply want a practical, fresh perspective (maybe you are a lifelong .45 caliber 1911 type and you are ready to try one of the "new" plastic guns) the information in this book is for you. We intend to simplify the decision-making process without skipping important details specific to your needs. We will break down the key elements of your decision-making to help you arrive at *The Point of the Gun*.

How this book is different than other firearm self defense books

The philosophy behind *The Point of the Gun* (TPOTG) offers that the best gun and caliber combo for self defense is the one you shoot accurately, consistently and with confidence- *and the one you have with you when you need it.* You don't need a classic 5 or 6 shot .44 Magnum revolver hand cannon to defend yourself against 2-legged threats (no offense, Inspector Callahan). Neither must you have a high capacity semi-auto, but that doesn't necessarily mean you shouldn't have either one. Both are excellent options.

S&W Model 29 .44 Magnum
All S&W images provided courtesy Smith and Wesson

Our recommendations and the information we share comes from a combined 70 years of buying, owning and selling thousands of guns. This includes guns for our personal use as well as the thousands of customers we've consulted and students we've trained. Additionally, we've done tests on hundreds of guns, the vast majority of which are firearms geared toward personal defense. These tests aren't the type where a manufacturer sends a gun in for a favorable review; these are guns we've owned or shot extensively and we've given an honest assessment as to their quality, reliability, and functionality. We've received no compensation for the tests or reviews but we've been rewarded with invaluable first hand knowledge and experience.

We don't believe a self defense firearm should be complicated or unnecessarily *accessorized*. We view firearms as self defense tools, designed for a specific, crucial task. While we enjoy and promote sport shooting, this book is focused on practical self defense firearms so we provide information and recommendations to help you select the right tool to protect yourself.

We encourage you to always have a gun with you whenever possible- this means concealed or open carry, in a purse or hip pack, or at least with you in your vehicle, even when you are just running errands. In spite of the understandable but often irrational fear of a loaded gun in today's society, there are very few things more useless than an unloaded gun, the exception being a loaded gun at home when you are a targeted victim elsewhere. If you don't have your gun with you when you most need it, what is the *point of your gun*?

According to legendary American firearms expert Jeff Cooper, "*The purpose of the pistol is to stop a fight that somebody else has started, almost always at very short range.*" The venerable Mr. Cooper knew that to defend yourself with a firearm, you need to have that firearm with you.

In the pages that follow, we'll go through the gun selection process with you, offering tips and suggestions for your consideration. We'll provide detailed descriptions of the types of handguns from which you will choose-**revolvers** and **semi-autos**. We'll go over the anatomy of each gun, the basic mechanics of how they work, the advantages and *perceived* disadvantages of both. We will provide a basic overview of ammunition calibers but we won't engage in a "best caliber" discussion because caliber selection is dependent upon numerous subjective factors personal to each shooter.

We'll discuss firearms for home defense. Whichever gun you choose for everyday carry (EDC) will also be an excellent choice for home defense but we'll also explore the advantages of long guns-**shotguns** and the often misunderstood "*evil black gun*," the **AR carbine**.

Hang around a gun shop or shooting range long enough, and you'll hear someone say, "The purpose of a handgun is to fight yourself to your long gun." This is the paraphrased wisdom of American firearms expert Clint Smith and alludes to the power and accuracy advantages of a long gun versus the handgun for home defense. We believe handguns and long guns are equally integral and wholly complementary to a home defense plan.

Since the *point of the gun* is to have it with you when you need it, we'll discuss methods of carry-holsters, purses or anything else that will keep your firearm close at hand at all times. A quality holster will be comfortable to wear, distribute the weight and size of your firearm, and thus encourage you to carry your firearm daily until you feel naked without it.

Part of a good holster or carry system is a good belt. A regular old belt just won't do-you need a belt built and designed to carry a gun. Beyond the belt, holsters can be worn on the chest, shoulders, and ankles. We'll concentrate on the best holster/carry options for defensive purposes, open and concealed.

For the ladies, we'll discuss purses. Yes, there are purses specifically designed to hold a firearm-in a *dedicated compartment* so that a gun will never get lost in the bottomless pit of a woman's purse. All joking aside, you can't afford to fumble in your purse, getting tangled with lipstick, compacts, cell phones and keys when you need your gun to defend yourself. A dedicated firearm compartment is not just for ease of access; it also keeps the gun cleaner, and is fundamentally *safer*.

We'll provide tips on shooting stance, grip ergonomics, operation and the ever-important maintenance of your firearm. Whichever gun you choose, it's important to note that it is a tool-nothing more, nothing less. Yes, guns can be romanticized as easily as vilified, but they are inanimate objects made animate only by the person pulling the trigger. Guns are manufactured parts of steel and polymer designed to accomplish a mechanical function. Like all tools, guns require basic maintenance to ensure they are in reliable, working, safe condition.

We want you to feel comfortable with your self defense guns; if you feel comfortable and confident, you'll practice shooting more and you will be better prepared if you ever need to use your gun in defense of you or your loved ones.

Over the course of years of consulting with new shooters on the purchase of firearms for self defense and instructing them how to use them, we've identified a few key commonalities that formulate the *Point of the Gun* approach:

The best firearm for self defense is a.) the one you have with you when you need it b.) the platform (revolver or semi-auto) you carry comfortably and thus consistently and c.) a size, weight, and caliber with which you can quickly, repeatedly and confidently hit your target- both in practice *and* under duress.

We will frequently reiterate one important *Point of the Gun* truism; simplicity. For self defense purposes, when the use of a firearm could literally mean the difference between your life and death, you cannot have any complications. Ease and proficiency of use will be facilitated by proper training, but also through the use of an unmodified firearm. This means that we will not advocate **tacticool** modifications-anything that unnecessarily accessorizes and does not markedly improve the defensive *practicality* and *dependability* of the gun.

Tacticool modifications include trigger jobs, expensive laser sights or optics, magazine extensions, etc... Yes, certain modifications like a trigger job can help enhance accuracy, and magazine extensions or tritium sights might improve one's grip, ammo capacity or sight/target acquisition. But as a rule, we staunchly promote the K.I.S.S method (Keep It Simple Shooter) when it comes to outfitting defensive carry guns.

Beyond straightforward, unaltered operation, a crucial argument for a stock firearm relates to the legal implications of using a weapon in self defense. In short, any modifications to a stock configuration firearm open the door for an anti-gun lawyer to argue that your modifications *prove* premeditation, that "you must have planned and therefore *wanted* to shoot someone." We know that's hogwash, but it's a troubling reality in today's lawsuit-crazed society.

We are not opposed to all aftermarket modifications of guns. Part of being a shooting enthusiast is the enjoyment of accessorizing your various guns to enhance your enjoyment for *recreational* purposes. However, self defense ***is not recreation***. Therefore, unless you have a disability that prevents you from using a firearm in its stock configuration, your daily carry gun should not be modified in the same way you might build out a competition handgun or a long range target rifle. A self defense gun will most likely be used in very close proximity to an attacker, often within arm's reach, but almost certainly within 20 feet. This defined range[2] is a critical consideration in the *legally defensible* use of a firearm in self defense.

This book is NOT a legal resource and should not be construed as offering legal advice. Learn your local and state laws and consult with an attorney if you want legal advice.

Jeff Cooper famously said *"Owning a handgun doesn't make you armed any more than owning a guitar makes you a musician."* His point is that one must prepare both physically and mentally, learning and shooting at the range as well as preparing your mind for the circumstances that might require you to use your weapon and *lethal force* in your own defense.

---

[2] There is no official, legally defined range that constitutes "self defense," but 21 feet is a generally cited distance. However, many factors are considered in a self defense shooting so it is imperative that gun owners learn their local and state laws.

The mental preparation is more important than the physical act of shooting, and there are no limitations preventing you from diligent mental preparation and awareness. This doesn't mean "looking for a reason" to use your firearm. It simply means cultivating an awareness of your surroundings in an effort to avoid being in the position of needing to use your firearm in self defense. That said, if trouble does come looking for you, you will be prepared.

This book is for you, the **law abiding citizen** ready to make an informed decision in choosing a gun for self defense. You've made the commitment to learn how to use a gun for your protection and that of your loved ones. Or, you may be an experienced shooter and you are ready to reevaluate your current Every Day Carry firearm. You will walk into your local gun shop *armed with practical knowledge* that will help you make the right choice for *you*.

You also know, as do we, that your right to buy a gun and exercise your natural, constitutional 2nd Amendment right to protect yourself is under constant threat of being taken away. You know now is the time to act.

And so, we are eager to explore with you the *Point of the Gun*.

CHAPTER 2

THE REVOLVER

No firearm has been more glorified, admired or immortalized than the revered revolver. Indeed, the revolver is considered the handgun that tamed the American West.[3] History provides images of Wyatt Earp's **Smith & Wesson Model 3 American** and Billy the Kid's **Colt model 1873** single action revolvers from the latter half of the 1800s, proof revolvers were used to great effect on both sides of the law. The revolver's effectiveness and dependability warranted its use as the police duty handgun of choice well into the 1990s. Revolvers are still a viable backup or off duty gun for law enforcement professionals today and remain a sound choice for personal self defense.

---

[3] The Winchester Model 1873 *rifle* is considered to be the gun that *won* the West

Smith and Wesson Model 3 *Colt Model 1873*
Courtesy of Smith and Wesson *Courtesy of NRA Museum*

Compared to earlier guns of all types, the revolver was a revolutionary design. Revolvers were the first *repeating* firearm, capable of successively firing multiple rounds without the need to reload bullet or powder between shots. In a revolver, the *cylinder* "revolves" (clockwise or counterclockwise depending upon the brand) to align each chamber with the entrance of the barrel. Revolvers typically come in "6-shooter" capacity models, but can have anywhere from five to eight round capacity. Certain .22 caliber revolvers have up to 10 round capacity.

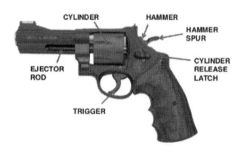

Revolver diagram
Courtesy of the National Rifle Association

The design of the revolver hasn't evolved much since its inception. Even with advances in manufacturing, materials and technology, the revolver remains relatively unchanged and is still known for unparalleled reliability and functionality. It is the easiest-to-use firearm for almost everybody-just point and pull the trigger. For these reasons, the revolver is one of the top considerations for self defense and every day carry.

The revolver is ubiquitous, with various frame sizes and capacity options from which to choose. Revolvers for daily carry range from the small, relatively lightweight .38 "snub nose," to the famed "Dirty Harry" .44 Magnum. Larger, heavy hunting revolvers include the .454 Casull and .500 S&W Magnum. Regardless of the size or caliber of a revolver, the mechanics of each are essentially the same, which makes their operation intuitive for most shooters.

As this book is focused on firearms for daily carry and self defense, we'll narrow our discussion to the lightweight "snubbies" and mid-size frame models in calibers .22, .38, 9mm (relatively new for revolvers), .357, and even .44 Magnum. For self defense purposes caliber is not the main consideration; *the ability to accurately hit your target is always the most important factor to consider when choosing a self defense carry gun*. This means that when shopping for a revolver (any handgun for that matter), you should handle and shoot a gun that interests you whenever possible. Many gun shops have a shooting range and a gun rental counter that will allow you to compare and contrast your various firearm options.

Revolvers come in three variants; **Single Action** (SA), **Double Action** (DA), and **Double Action Only** (DAO).

In a *Single Action* revolver the shooter manually cocks (pulls back) the hammer, either with a thumb from the support or strong hand. The *strong hand* is your dominant hand with which you will hold the gun and pull the trigger. Your *support hand* is the opposite hand, which provides extra support when shooting two-handed. The *hammer* is the part of the revolver that strikes the firing pin when the trigger is pulled. The *firing pin* is what hits the primer of the *cartridge* (ammunition), igniting the *propellant* (gun powder) which in turn "fires" the bullet. A single action revolver will not operate just by pulling the trigger; it must be manually cocked for it to shoot.

In a **Double Action** revolver, the action of cocking the hammer can be done in two ways; manually or by simply pulling the trigger. Pulling the trigger cocks *and* releases the hammer, so a DA *trigger pull* (the amount of effort or force required to pull the trigger and measured in *pounds* of pressure) is noticeably more than that of a SA revolver. This is what is known as a "heavier" trigger pull. So, in a DA revolver, there are two (double) actions that will cock the hammer.

SINGLE-ACTION REVOLVER
THE TRIGGER PERFORMS A SINGLE ACTION: RELEASING THE HAMMER. THE HAMMER MUST BE MANUALLY COCKED FOR EACH SHOT.

DOUBLE-ACTION REVOLVER
THE TRIGGER PERFORMS TWO TASKS: BOTH COCKING AND RELEASING THE HAMMER. MOST DOUBLE-ACTION REVOLVERS CAN ALSO BE FIRED IN THE SINGLE-ACTION MODE.

SA/DA

Double Action Only (DAO) revolvers lack the hardware that allows the hammer to be manually locked in the cocked position. DAO revolvers typically have a *bobbed* or internal hammer. The DAO revolver mechanism means the trigger pull will always be uniformly heavier than a single action. It also means there is no hammer to snag on a pocket, shirt, or other piece of clothing when drawing your weapon. An example of a DAO revolver is the Smith and Wesson (S&W) model 642 snub nose.

S&W J-frame Model 642 .38 caliber
Note the absence of an exposed hammer
All S&W firearm images courtesy of Smith and Wesson

What's better for everyday carry self defense purposes-a SA, DA, or DAO revolver? DA and DAO revolvers are generally preferred because they don't require the shooter to manually cock the hammer. Pulling back the hammer takes additional time as well as motor skill memory and requires extensive training to perform safely. If you have to defend yourself with a firearm, the fewer the steps required, the fewer the possibilities for something to go wrong.

Some of the best small frame snub nosed, or short barreled revolvers, are DAO. They have a slightly heavier trigger pull (compared to a SA) but in a stressful situation you won't be thinking about the extra "pounds" you need to pull. You'll just point at the offending target and pull the trigger with more adrenaline-infused strength than you even knew you had. The most famous of the small framed "snubbies" are the Smith and Wesson "J-frame" revolvers like the Model 642 pictured above. They are lightweight and can be safely carried in a pocket.

Another significant benefit of the revolver is that it requires no disassembly for basic maintenance and cleaning. The two main block components of a modern revolver-the *frame* and the *cylinder*-are fixed to one another. To clean and lube the gun, you activate the cylinder release *latch* or *button* and the cylinder will pop to the side of the gun, still attached. With practice, you can completely clean a revolver after shooting in less than ten minutes. If you shoot a lot, quick and easy cleaning is a big advantage. Ease of maintenance will inspire you to practice more, which is a GREAT thing for your confidence and shooting proficiency.

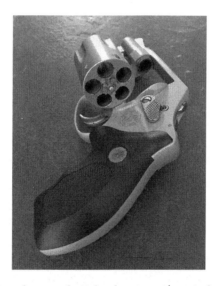

Revolver with Cylinder open & attached

In a revolver all *cartridges* are enclosed in the revolver's cylinder, rather than a *magazine* (discussed in the next chapter). Each trigger pull will discharge a round until all rounds have been fired. They cylinder will continue to rotate with each trigger pull, even if all cartridges have been fired.

The more you shoot, the faster you'll learn and appreciate that lack of complexity equates to increased safety. Revolvers do not have a **mechanical safety** device (as found on a 1911 semi-auto for example). Double Action revolvers do have the tactile benefit of requiring a deliberate pull of the "heavier" trigger for a round to be discharged. Thus, your own judgement and *trigger finger discipline* (never allow your finger on the trigger until you are absolutely ready to shoot) are the collective safety.

Modern revolvers are generally manufactured from steel and metal alloys such as scandium, titanium, and aluminum, and many are now made in polymer (lightweight durable plastic). Bear in mind that most of the lighter weight materials won't absorb recoil as well as steel (polymer does flex a bit), but since they are lighter in weight, they will be far more comfortable to carry for long periods of time. Since you are likely to do far more carrying than shooting (aside from practicing) you have to decide what's a more important trade-off.

Depending upon the metal or alloy of the firearm, you'll usually have a choice between stainless steel, blued, or polymer. Stainless steel is highly corrosion resistant and won't rust as long as it is properly maintained. A *blued* gun will have black or indigo color; bluing is an electrochemical process to aid against rust and scratching. Polymer may be black or whatever new color a manufacturer has decided to produce. Polymer itself is 100% corrosion resistant. Regardless of the material construction, most modern revolver materials are relatively low maintenance, so what you choose will likely come down to personal taste.

The general simplicity of a revolver means it is also one of the easiest guns to learn to shoot competently. Most new shooters figure out how to shoot a revolver quickly and the short operational learning curve will inspire confidence just as fast. The revolver is truly an all-in-one self defense firearm.

Familiarize yourself with the names of some of the more popular modern revolver brands; they are popular because of their longstanding tradition of quality and reliability. Consequently, these are some of the most commercially available and trustworthy brands.

Smith and Wesson (S&W)

Ruger

Dan Wesson (CZ-USA)

Charter Arms

*Colt Manufacturing

Ruger LCR .38 SPL +P

Image courtesy of Sturm, Ruger & Co. Inc

Charter Arms Bulldog .44 SPL

Image courtesy of Charter Arms

What you purchase is up to you, but we highly encourage you to consider S&W, Ruger and Charter Arms, for all three brands have a wide variety of options in action, size and caliber at competitive prices.

Dan Wesson is the great grandson of S&W founder D.B. Wesson, so he's got high quality revolver manufacturing in his blood. His models are manufactured and sold through Czech firearm company CZ (Česká zbrojovka). Dan Wesson revolvers are pricey and on the larger side, so while they are fantastic, high quality and reliable for home defense (HD) and target shooting, they are not ideal for carry when compared to the less expensive, high quality, smaller and lighter options.

We mention Colt Manufacturing because of their famed history in producing legendary revolvers. As of this printing, Colt is set to re-enter the market but we can't advocate for their new offerings without legitimate testing and longer term use. We're hopeful however that this iconic brand will become a major player in the revolver market again.

Be prepared to pay **$400-$900** for a dependable Everyday Carry revolver. You can possibly find used revolvers for a lower price, but one of the great selling points of quality revolvers, especially those made of steel, is that they don't lose much in resale or performance value over time, provided they are well maintained.

By now you've got a pretty comprehensive overview the revolver and why it is a great choice, if not ideal, for everyday carry and personal defense.

CHAPTER 3

SEMI-AUTOMATIC HANDGUNS

Next we'll explore the *auto loading,* or *semi-automatic* handgun.

Semi-automatic handguns are the preferred duty sidearm of almost all every military and police force in the world. Considering what we just learned about the "bulletproof" reliability and functionality of the revolver, why is the semi-auto so prevalent with fighting men and women and law enforcement personnel?

The main reason is ammunition *capacity*; semi-autos generally have a higher capacity than revolvers, on average 10-18 rounds depending on the make, size and caliber of the firearm. When engaging multiple targets, capacity can be *almost* as important as shot placement. Semi-autos also utilize ammunition *magazines* (the apparatus that holds and feeds ammunition to the firearm) allowing the shooter rapid reloading with another 10-20 rounds to put on target.

As we discuss semi-auto handguns, it's important to pause to make a very crucial distinction between the terms fully automatic and semi-automatic. Auto loading firearms can be both ***full-auto*** and ***semi-auto***.

In a *fully automatic* firearm, when the trigger is pulled and held, rounds will continue to fire until the trigger is released (or the magazine is empty). This is what is often portrayed in Hollywood as a "machine gun" or epitomized by the famous Uzi and MAC-10 pistols. Full-autos typically have a *fire selector switch* to allow for 3 round bursts, or fully-automatic discharge of the rounds until the trigger is released.

Fully automatic firearms are only available to private citizens after completion of intensive paperwork, often a year long background check and waiting period, and an expensive tax stamp. Fully automatic firearms are not legal in all states.

In a semi-auto (handgun or rifle) a single pull of the trigger will fire a single round. The trigger must be pulled successively to fire multiple rounds, one at a time. The vast majority of *legally* owned firearms in the United States are *semi-automatic*.

A semi-auto handgun operates differently than a revolver. The first round is *chambered* by pulling back on the *slide*-this process is called "racking" the slide. When the trigger of a semi-auto is pulled, the hammer or internal striker hits the firing pin similarly to a revolver. But after the round is fired from a semi-auto, the gasses expelled by the spent cartridge move the slide rearward, eject the *shell casing* of the cartridge and almost simultaneously reload the next cartridge (which was pushed up into the loading position by a spring in the magazine). This process is repeated each time the trigger is pulled and continues until the last round is fired, whereupon the *slide lock/slide stop lever* (on *most* semi autos) holds the slide in an open position, ready for the next magazine to be inserted into the handgun.

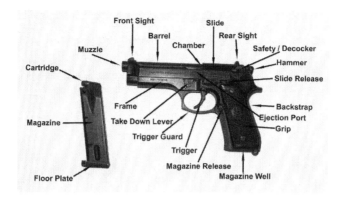

Semi-automatic pistol + magazine

Image courtesy of the NRA

Right away you'll note the relatively more complicated design, operation and the higher number of external operating components of most semi-autos compared to revolvers. This isn't a positive or a negative per se, but something to be considered in your overall evaluation of which is more appropriate *for you*.

History of the semi-automatic handgun:

The manufacture of high capacity auto loaders began with larger weapons like the recoil-operated machine gun, designed in 1883 by American-born British inventor Hiram Maxim. It wasn't long before inventors saw the opportunity to apply the idea of an auto loading weapon to the manufacture of handguns, and by 1892 the first semi-automatic pistol was created by Austrian inventor Joseph Laumann. By 1896, German Paul Mauser (of the Mauser rifle fame) introduced his C96 semi-automatic pistol which quickly became the highest capacity commercially produced semi-auto handgun through the turn of the century.

Enter American John Browning. Born in Ogden, Utah in 1855, Browning designed the first semi-automatic handgun manufactured by

Belgian firm Fabrique Nationale (FN), also in 1896. In the early years of the 1900s Browning designed his famous single action .45 ACP which was officially adopted by the United States military in 1911. Hence, the Browning Model 1911 was born, and it is still widely used and revered today by militaries and loyal civilians alike. A true **1911** is a single action semi-auto but the 1911 moniker is often used to describe many of the hammer fired semi-auto handguns today.

Hammer fired and Striker fired semi-autos

A *hammer fired* semi auto refers to the trigger and mechanism that strikes the firing pin, and is commonly known as double/single action firearm (similar to a revolver). In a hammer fired semi auto, the first trigger pull is a long (heavy) pull that both cocks and releases the hammer to engage the firing pin. Subsequent trigger pulls are about half the "weight" of the first pull as the hammer is already immediately re-cocked and ready to fire following the first discharge. Thus, a hammer fired semi-auto has two different trigger pull weights.

Hammer fired handguns often have a safety mechanism that prevents the trigger and hammer action of engaging the firing pin. When the safety is engaged the firearm can be carried loaded (round in the chamber), hammer back, and ready to fire. The safety must be disengaged before the gun will fire. With training, this can be accomplished quickly in a self defense situation, but it is also an extra step and a differentiating factor from a striker fired handgun or a double action hammer fired handgun that lack safeties.

Modern hammer fired handguns are often made mostly of metal, but companies like Heckler and Koch do manufacture polymer framed hammer fired firearms like the P30 and HK45.

Hammer fired semi-automatic

Image courtesy of NRA

Striker fired handguns lack both a double action trigger as well as a hammer. In most striker fired handguns, once the slide is racked and a round is chambered, the striker, or firing "pin," is pulled back and held in place by a *sear*. The firing pin is encased in a high tension spring. The trigger pull is consistent from the first to the last. When the uniform, single action trigger is pulled, the firing pin directly strikes the base of the loaded round, activating the primer and igniting the propellant, thereby discharging the round.

Striker fired semi-auto

Image courtesy of Glock

Striker fired guns do not have a physical external safety mechanism, but this doesn't mean they are unsafe compared to hammer fire guns. Indeed, most striker fire guns made by companies like Glock, Sig Sauer and Heckler and Koch (H&K) utilize multiple trigger and internal safety mechanisms, all of which prevent the firearm from discharging a round accidentally, i.e. by dropping the gun. The responsibility for safe carry and use of a striker fire handgun rests completely with the shooter, mandating trigger finger discipline and correct safety precautions while loading, unloading, holstering and unholstering, and cleaning.

The weight difference between hammer fire and striker fire guns is not just about fewer internal moving parts. Most striker fire guns today are polymer framed as opposed to metal. The polymer used to manufacture gun frames is a hard, durable plastic material that is considerably lighter in weight than metal, but also equal in strength and durability. Polymer doesn't rust and is completely corrosion resistant.

Striker fire guns do have metal parts, including the slide and important internal components, but polymer striker fire handguns are essentially half the weight of their typically metal hammer fire counterparts. The lighter weight and density of the polymer may not soak up recoil like a heavier mostly-metal gun, but *recoil sensitivity* is a subjective factor. Polymer does flex however, and absorbs some felt recoil upon firing.

Both hammer and striker fired semi-automatic firearms utilize magazines to house and feed them ammo. Magazines are often incorrectly referred to as "clips." Magazines have a spring that pushes up and feeds the ammunition (cartridges) into the gun itself. Clips have no spring, and simply hold the cartridges in place for sequential feeding. The term "clip" is a historical holdover from guns like the venerable M1 Garand (WWII, Korean War, early part of Vietnam) which was fed by clips holding .30 caliber ammunition. So if you want avoid looking like a newbie at your gun shop, always say "magazine" when asking questions like- "How many rounds does the *magazine* of this handgun hold?"

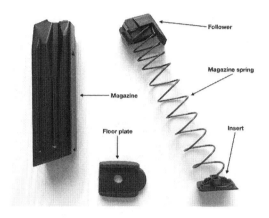

Magazine components

Magazine cutaway
Courtesy of the National Rifle Association

Magazines are comprised of the body of the magazine, a *spring* held in place by the *base or floor plate*, and a magazine *follower*. The follower rests on top of the spring and is designed with the proper geometry to feed the cartridges at the necessary angle into the chamber. The last round in a magazine sits directly on the follower while all the others sit on top of each other. So the last round is "followed" by this component, which is under decreasing spring tension with each successive round fired.

Magazines are either *single stack* or *double stack*. Single stack magazines, typical of 1911 style and subcompact semi-autos, have all the rounds in a vertical line and typically have up to an 8 round capacity. Double stack magazine rounds are in two staggered "columns" and are most often used in high capacity semi autos. Double stack magazines are wider in order to accommodate the two columns. Double stack magazines generally hold twice the capacity of a single stack magazine depending upon the caliber of the cartridge and size of the frame (subcompact, compact, full size).

Single stack and double stack magazine

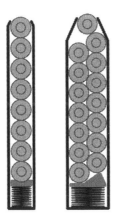

Courtesy of NRA

Cost of semi auto handguns

Expect to pay about the same for a quality personal defense semi-auto as you would for a quality personal defense revolver. Pricing for self defense oriented semi-auto handguns is in the range of $450 to

$900, and you'll pay more (sometimes quite a bit more) for a hammer fired 1911 type.

Some of the semi-auto brands you'll see at your local gun shop will include **Glock, Sig Sauer, FN** Herstal, **Heckler and Koch (HK), Smith & Wesson, Springfield Armory, CZ-USA, Ruger, Beretta, Browning, Colt, Walther, Kahr** and **Kimber.**

As with revolvers, your ultimate decision will come down to ergonomics, notably in terms of grip, weight, and overall balance in your hand-especially with *a fully loaded magazine, which adds significant weight* compared to an empty magazine. You have many capacity options from which to choose, and with some semi autos you don't necessarily have to sacrifice capacity for ease of carry and concealability.

Finally, if you have a chance to shoot before buying, it's important to understand how all the ergonomics contribute to your ability to hit the target at the range and during a stressful situation. Sometimes a gun feels better and thus will shoot better for one individual but not another. Sometimes a gun may feel awkward at first, but you may shoot more accurately with it than another that *feels* better *in the hand.*

Now you understand the basics of both revolvers and semi autos. So which is "better?" The more relevant question asks which is better for *you*? We'll discuss revolvers and semi autos and consider the comparative pros and cons of each next.

CHAPTER 4

COMPARING REVOLVERS AND SEMI-AUTOS FOR EDC

There is not a one-size-fits-all *people* or *scenario* handgun. Therefore, it's important to consider a short list of criteria when determining which defensive handgun and platform will best fit the majority of your needs. Different handguns will cover overlapping needs, but you should make your decision on your primary need-in this case *self defense*-for your personal protection firearm. *Do not settle* for any aspect of your self defense firearm that would compromise your ability to hit your target **quickly**, **accurately**, and **repeatedly**.

The good news is that choosing a gun from behind a glass gun counter is not as daunting as say, choosing a bottle of wine at the grocery store, trying to select from the many different varietals, regions, and price points. The differences in the mechanics, operation and price between revolvers and semi autos are much easier to identify and comprehend. You can't really make a wrong choice-*unless you ignore the basics of personal* ergonomics like grip, weight, balance, recoil, and your ability to shoot accurately and confidently with a particular firearm. But, your hand and physical strength is unique to you, which means your grip is also unique to you. So the *fit* of the gun to your hand will also be specific to you.

You've gained a general understanding of revolvers and semi autos from the previous chapters. You now have a basic comprehension of their operation-Single Action vs. Double Action, cylinder-fed vs. auto loading by magazine, hammer fired vs. striker fired, metal frame vs. polymer. Most importantly, you now appreciate that *only you* can determine what the most important attributes of any firearm mean to you as you make your decision.

So how should you go about determining what characteristics are most important to you in deciding which gun to choose for self defense? We'll explore the following factors to demonstrate how revolvers stack up with semi-autos, and vice versa. It's a report card of sorts, but you determine the final "grade" based on your needs and desires.

Capacity

To keep things simple, let's start with what is probably the biggest difference between revolvers and semi autos-**capacity**. Capacity is a significant differentiating factor for consideration. Semi autos as a *general* rule carry more rounds than revolvers. As you know, defensive carry revolvers carry between 5-8 rounds. While a subcompact single stack semi-auto carries 6 rounds and a hammer fired 1911 style semi auto will likely have only 8 rounds, a similar mid to full sized striker fired semi-auto will often carry twice as many or more. So as a *general rule*, semi autos have an edge in capacity over revolvers.

Cylinder capacity

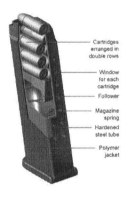

Magazine capacity

Image courtesy of Glock

For self defense purposes, does capacity really matter that much? If you spend some time researching the numerous internet forums dedicated to gun discussion, you'll be led to believe that capacity is king for self defense-for those moments when you are confronted by multiple terrorists or a gang of armed thieves. Unfortunately, while either scenario might be more of a (remote) statistical possibility today than at any other time in our history, it is still improbable in your day to day life.

While contemplating capacity, it's also worth considering the distance within which you'll most likely need to defend yourself, or of equal importance what is considered a *legally defensible distance* in a self defense situation. The generally accepted range within which may constitute an act of self defense with a firearm is a few inches up to 21 feet. This is why most gun ranges have the first red line across the floor at 7 yards.

21 feet is not very far. The average person can close this distance in under 2 seconds.[4] So for you to claim self defense, you will *generally* be held to a standard of that short distance within which you can argue using your firearm in self defense. Anything further and opposing lawyers will argue that you could have taken a number of other measures to get away from the "poor victim criminal" who tried to rob, maim, or kill you.

How many rounds do you need to *stop the threat* at 7 yards? One? Two? Ten? More? A rapidly *moving-toward-you* threat, not a standing still piece of paper hanging innocuously at the range. This moving-toward-you threat has a knife, gun, or other object that can ruin your life. Now you are beginning to see why shot placement is more important than capacity, caliber, or just about any other factor when it comes to stopping the threat.

Your goal in using a firearm for self defense is *not to kill*. It is *not to wound*. It is *not to warn* your attacker. Your only objective (if you cannot

---

[4] The Tueller Drill, created by Sergeant Dennis Tueller of the Salt Lake City Police Department sought to determine how quickly an attacking assailant with a knife could cover 21 feet. Volunteer participants averaged 1.5 seconds, quantifying a legitimate "danger zone" within which an assailant can be determined to be an imminent, grave threat.

get away safely) must be to **STOP THE THREAT**. How many rounds do you need to stop the threat? If you hit center mass to the heart, head or central nervous system (CNS) you may only need one round. But in a stress situation where your life is in jeopardy, you might be pulling the trigger as fast as you can rather than analyzing if your first shot did the trick or if you need a few more. With a single threat (bad guy) the whole incident will likely be over in mere seconds, well before your brain can catch up to the action.

Nobody can armchair quarterback a future hypothetical scenario to know definitively how many rounds would be required in a self defense situation involving a firearm. However, if you only need a round or two to STOP THE THREAT, you aren't at a disadvantage in having a high capacity handgun. You don't need to shoot all of the rounds just because you have them. But, if you do require more rounds than a revolver affords, say, for multiple threats, a semi-auto *generally* offers a higher capacity option. Should you find yourself in the aforementioned (however improbable) multiple terrorist scenario discussed above (as has happened recently in Europe as well as the United States), more rounds will give you a better fighting chance to get away and ultimately save your life.

Capacity- advantage semi auto

Note on statistics: there are many statistics on firearm use for self defense, including justifiable shootings, crime rates, etc… FBI statistics tend to be the most reliable, but even the most frequently cited FBI data primarily discusses the use of firearms in law enforcement (cop vs. criminal), not citizen self defense situations. Instead of relying on statistics, you need to train consistently with your firearm. Training and awareness go a long way toward keeping you from becoming a statistic yourself. Of parallel importance, you must learn and stay current in your knowledge of your state and local laws.

Operation

Simplicity, or ease of operation is another obvious criterion upon which to compare revolvers and semi autos. This is a pretty clear cut advantage of the revolver. Granted, thorough and disciplined practice narrows the difference between the two, but what could be simpler than pointing a revolver, pulling the trigger and having the gun go bang? In a revolver, there's no magazine to load, no racking of the slide to chamber a round, and no disengagement of a safety mechanism.

That said, in practice, revolver ease of operation comes with one perceptible drawback for some shooters- the heavier trigger pull. The full trigger pull on a DA or DAO revolver (without the hammer having been manually cocked) will always be heavier in a revolver (approximately 12 lbs. vs. 5-7lbs in *striker fired* semi autos, or the second trigger pull in a *hammer fired* semi auto). So a revolver does require a stronger trigger finger. But, in a high stress situation, adrenaline is likely going to provide all the extra strength for most people to pull the extra 5-7 lbs. of revolver trigger.

The heavier trigger pull is also a safety benefit; a heavier trigger pull requires that you "mean it" when you pull the trigger. It's highly unlikely that you could inadvertently fire the gun by simply snagging it on a pants or coat pocket. While your finger should never be on the trigger unless you intend to fire the gun, a heavier pull guards against a "nervous" finger. Since a revolver is always "chambered" and ready to fire, one handed operation is always an option (although two hands are desirable whenever possible as both aid in accuracy and control).

Successful discharge of a round with a revolver is not affected by a weak grip or *limp wristing*. Limp wristing typically occurs when the shooter doesn't have a firm or secure enough grip on a firearm while shooting and is most commonly associated with semi-autos. Limp wristing can cause a round to be *out of battery* (the round does not load into the chamber completely and thus will not fire). This simply won't happen with a revolver.

Another advantage of revolvers is that they do not have a magazine that can jam, break, or fall out of the gun if not seated properly. Whereas a semi-auto can experience a failure to feed (FTF) which necessitates a two-handed manual clearing of the chamber and re-rack of the slide, with a revolver one must only continue to pull the trigger to cycle through to the next round.

Operation-advantage revolver

Carryability/concealability

Now things start to get a little murky. After comparing capacity and ease of operation in revolvers vs. semi autos, the gap between the perceived advantages and disadvantages narrows significantly. This is actually good news since it further underscores the reality that you cannot make a wrong choice between the two.

In discussing whether a revolver or semi auto is easier to carry and conceal, we're considering factors like size, weight, and to some degree shape. Each factor is a consideration that determines if the firearm can be easily and perhaps unobtrusively carried for long periods of time. Of course in a purse or waist pack one can carry a firearm indefinitely with little discomfort. But worn in a holster (or carried in a pocket), size and weight of the firearm matter. And if you want to be truly inconspicuous, "*printing*" (the visible outline of your firearm under your clothing) is another consideration. When someone says something like "My Glock 17 (full frame 9mm semi auto) prints in the back," they mean the bottom of the grip pokes into their clothing and shows the protrusion- a telltale giveaway that they are carrying a firearm.

In open-carry jurisdictions, where the visible and "open" carry of a firearm is legal, printing isn't that big of a deal. However, carrying concealed is done for reasons we'll discuss in greater detail later.

Nowadays, it has become increasingly easy to conceal a revolver or a semi-auto. Advances in materials and the manufacturing process mean that polymer is no longer only the domain of semi-autos. Small frame Ruger revolvers like the LCR series offer versatility and firepower along with excellent concealability. Additionally, the lightweight metal alloys like Scandium and Titanium mean that you don't need to choose a snubbie if you want to carry a revolver. The S&W .44 Magnum model 329PD, while a large frame revolver, weighs a feathery 25 oz. unloaded- it's a Scandium alloy frame with a Titanium alloy cylinder! But even the small to medium steel frame revolvers are relatively lightweight with numerous aftermarket holster options from which to choose.

S&W 329 PD .44 Magnum

Generally speaking, any revolver with more than a 5-round capacity is going to be about the same weight if not slightly heavier than a *subcompact* semi auto. The Sig Sauer P238 semi auto in .380 caliber is 5.5 inches "tall" (measured bottom of the grip to the top of the slide) and tips the scales at just under a pound. So when you start getting into the medium sized metal framed revolvers, their *compact* semi auto brethren are going to be equal in weight *or lighter*, even fully loaded with 10 rounds or more in the magazines.

So capacity aside, you might see a weight ratio advantage with subcompact to compact polymer semi autos, with either single or double stack magazines. The famed Glock 19 in 9mm, which is technically almost a full frame semi auto has a capacity of 15+1 (in the chamber) and weighs a little over 30 oz loaded- that's barely 5 oz heavier than the *unloaded* Scandium/Titaniam full frame S&W 329PD revolver, yet the Glock has 10 more rounds of capacity (albeit in a smaller caliber)!

Glock 19 9mm

Image provided courtesy of Glock

Given the range of sizes, widths, loaded weights, materials, grips and barrel lengths, you'll need to prioritize which attributes are most important to you in your handgun selection. In terms of comfort, i.e., while driving or sitting, the grip length is actually going to be one of the biggest factors. Most people only think of carrying their gun while standing and moving. But you will actually also be sitting quite a lot- on a couch, chair, or car seat while wearing too- and a gun will let you know quickly if it is uncomfortable or unmanageably "too big" for EDC.

Ultimately, both revolvers and semi autos can be easily carried and concealed. Carryability depends almost entirely on the size, materials, and caliber you want to shoot. Why does caliber play into the equation? Only because larger calibers require a larger overall gun size. In the case of .38 vs. 9mm it may not make much difference. But if you jump to .45 or 10mm, a "thicker" gun is required to accommodate the width/diameter of the larger cartridges. So the key is to balance all of the requirements most important to you, which may require a compromise or trade-off here and there.

Remember, shot placement is still the most important factor, so whatever constitutes a compromise in your selection, just make sure you never compromise your ability to shoot the firearm accurately!

Carryability and Concealability- Draw

Power

Power is contentious term when deciding on a firearm. Few things will start a "caliber war" quicker than mentioning the phrase "*stopping power.*" Stopping power is often cited to validate someone's opinion on the *best* caliber. You know by now that stopping power has more to do with shot placement than caliber.

As part of your analysis to determine which handgun you choose, power should be lower on your list of priorities. It's absolutely an important *consideration*, but advances in ballistic performance in modern ammunition available today affords you the option of carrying a traditionally "lower" power cartridge like the 9mm rather than having to carry bigger calibers like the tried and true .357 and .45.

Some advocates argue that revolvers are more "powerful" than semi-autos. Ballistically speaking, *power* is determined by "size" of caliber (diameter of the cartridge), velocity, and penetration (bullet weight and construction). Since *ballistic performance* is generally enhanced in firearms with longer barrels (minimum 3-4 inches), we don't promote revolver "power" as an advantage of revolvers for everyday defensive carry, since you won't likely be *carrying* a revolver with a barrel longer than 4 inches as your EDC firearm. For a home defense firearm though, you have the option and advantage of using a full sized, longer barrelled revolver on the nightstand or in a drawer.

Caliber "power" is measured and quantified in bullet **feet per second** (velocity from the barrel), foot-pounds of energy delivered on target, size of the hole on target, and penetration (wound channel into the target). Factors that influence power are bullet weight (measured in "grains") and whether or not the bullet is solid, copper cast, heavy cast, hollow point, jacketed hollow point, semi-jacketed hollow point, lead semi-wadcutter hollow point, full metal jacket, and so on.

There are many variables that determine handgun caliber power but it's not necessary to go into them here, especially since they are not revolver or semi auto contingent. Some calibers are more ballistically "barrel length sensitive" meaning that their performance is influenced greatly by barrel length-.357 is one such caliber. But a .357 shot through a snub barrel revolver still packs an effective wallop on target at self defense ranges.

For defense against people, jacketed hollow points (JHP) offer maximum expansion and *threat-stopping* tissue disruption that transfers the bulk of the bullet's kinetic energy directly into the target. Hollow points usually stop within the target body, and thus generally present less of an over-penetration threat to innocent bystanders. Innocent bystanders are more likely to be struck by a "miss" than they are to be hit by an over-penetrating bullet.

While one could argue that a higher capacity firearm has more "power" than a revolver in the equivalent caliber, such an assertion does not take into account all the variables necessary to solidify capacity as a power advantage for an everyday carry handgun. This is one reason we suggest that power should be lower on your list of selection priorities (much lower than shot placement, shot placement and shot placement!).

Power- Draw

Maintenance

It is the obligation of the responsible gun owner and CCW license holder to practice with his or her firearm, to be competent in its use, and accurate in his or her ability to hit the intended target. This requires practice. Consequently, it is also the obligation of the responsible gun owner to clean and maintain his or her firearm, to ensure that it is in safe, working condition at all times.

For basic cleaning and maintenance, the revolver has two components-the cylinder and the frame (which includes the barrel). Both are fixed to one another so there's no taking it apart or separating the pieces from each other.

Even one of the least complicated semi autos- Glock 17 or variants -breaks down into 5 separate parts for basic maintenance. Semi-autos also have more exposed internal components that require attention.

Cleaning a revolver is uncomplicated. After ensuring it is unloaded, activate the cylinder release, and pop the cylinder to the side. Clean the obvious powder residue off the frame with solvent or lube, run a bore brush or other apparatus with a lubed cloth patch through the barrel and each cylinder chamber, clean the ejector rod, extractor and ratchet, repeat with a dry patch, close the cylinder and you're done. That's it. For this reason, revolvers have a slight edge over semi-autos when it comes to maintenance.

It's not that a semi-auto is difficult to maintain, even with a handful more accessible parts. It's just that overall process of maintaining a revolver is so straightforward. There are no parts to lose while cleaning a revolver because everything stays together as one piece.

In a semi-auto, the firearm breaks down into its basic 5 or more components for cleaning. To clean it, ensure it is unloaded, wipe down each individual part, lube and clean each individual part with a moist (cleaner/lubricant) patch, wipe each individual part again with a dry patch, and then lube the 6 or more spots on which the slide rides the frame, along with a couple other key areas that generally see the most wear and tear. Reassemble all the parts, rack the slide and dry fire (no round or magazine).

With practice, cleaning a semi auto is not a remotely difficult or time consuming task. It is just a marginally more involved process than cleaning a revolver since semi auto components break down separately from one another.

Maintenance-advantage revolver

So in the general comparison above, does the 2-1 "score" of revolvers over semi-autos mean that revolvers are the best choice for an everyday self defense firearm? Yes for some people, and no for others. You know by now that the most important factors in choosing a firearm are purely subjective- and must advance your ability to be *competent, confident,* and *consistent* in your shooting.

It is necessary to note that with practice and everyday carry, you may come to realize certain factors are more important than you thought they were when you first set out to purchase a self defense firearm, while other factors may become less important to you. If this leads you to buy another gun, consider that you are just buying another tool in which you'll have more confidence. Whether that means you sell the first, or keep it for your nightstand at home, it is up to you to decide.

There is no one-size-fits-all handgun; there is only the size that best fits *your* needs and desires. Remember also, you don't wear the same clothes every day, so it's ok to have more than one gun!

CHAPTER 5

AMMUNITION BASICS

This chapter will familiarize you with the anatomy of a cartridge, including the various components that put the "bang" into whatever caliber you are shooting. Whether it's a speedy .22 Long Rifle or the muscular .44 Magnum, the general components that make up a cartridge are the same.

A *rimfire cartridge* (like a .22 caliber) ignites when the firing pin strikes the rim of the base of the cartridge, while in a *centerfire cartridge* the firing pin strikes the center of the cartridge. Most cartridges used for self defense are centerfire.

Rimfire vs. Centerfire

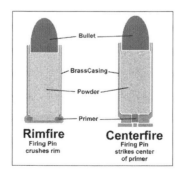

Image courtesy of the National Rifle Association (or NRA)

From the bottom to the top, a cartridge is comprised of the *primer*, *gunpowder*, *casing*, and *bullet*. The firing pin strikes the **primer cup** which is filled with a *priming compound*- the chemical mixture that sparks when struck. In a rimfire cartridge, typically in the .22 caliber, the priming compound is in the rim of the cartridge; in a centerfire cartridge it is in, you guessed it, the center. This spark or flame shoots through the **flash hole** and ignites the **gunpowder**, which in turn propels the **bullet** out of the barrel.

Image courtesy of the National Rifle Association

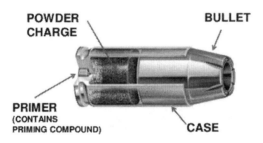

The caliber marking is designated on the cartridge *head*. Aside from visually identifying caliber by size, you can always confirm by looking at the *head stamp*.

Cartridge head stamp

Image courtesy of the National Rifle Association

The cartridge *casing* is the metal housing that contains all the other components. The casing is usually made of brass, but it can also be made of aluminum or steel. Some cases are nickel plated for corrosion resistance and ease of ejection. When shooting at a range, it isn't uncommon to see fellow shooters picking up their spent "brass" from the ground. These folks are most likely "*reloaders*" or "*handloaders*" and they reload their brass with the aforementioned components to make cartridges to their desired specifications.

Reloading requires specialized equipment that measures gunpowder, casing diameter, and "ingredients" such as primers, bullets etc... The equipment is used to fuse all the components of a cartridge together. One advantage of reloading is that over time, and if you shoot *a lot*, the cost per cartridge becomes quite inexpensive.

Although reloading is quite common and can be fun and cost effective for gun enthusiasts, it's not something we recommend for new shooters. Modern ammunition for defensive purposes is very good and made to precise specifications and while some calibers are more expensive to produce, the primary *practice* cartridges are relatively inexpensive. Plus, if done improperly, reloading can be dangerous. If the gunpowder is not measured precisely, excessive pressure can result causing a catastrophic failure of the firearm and potential injury to the shooter.

Revolver destroyed by improperly measured reload ammunition
Note the ruptured cylinder chamber and completely missing barrel

Defensive ammunition will cost more than practice ammunition, but you won't be shooting much of your defensive ammunition (other than a few rounds just to be certain you are proficient with it). You don't "discount" the value of your life, so just as you should spend smart money on a high quality firearm, you should also buy high quality ammunition for self defense.

There are minor differences between revolver cartridges and semi-automatic cartridges. In a revolver cartridge, the *base of the cartridge* is wider in diameter than the shell casing. This keeps the cartridge from falling into the cylinder, and allows for easy extraction by the ejector rod/extractor of the revolver. In a revolver cartridge the *bullet diameter* is wider than the *inside* of the shell casing so the bullet is pressed and held into place.

In a semi auto cartridge, the base diameter is essentially the same as the diameter of the casing, but it has a recessed groove around the base that the semi auto extractor "grabs" to eject the spent cartridge.

Another important term to know is *jacketing*. In discussing bullets, you'll frequently hear descriptors like *full metal jacket* (FMJ) and *jacketed hollow point* (JHP). The core of a jacketed bullet is often a soft metal (usually lead) encased in a gilding metal, which is simply a copper alloy that is harder than the core.

Full Metal Jacket cartridge

The biggest benefit to the jacket is that it is less susceptible to deformation on impact. Jacketing also aids in the feeding of the round into the chamber. Jacketed (non-hollow point) bullets are usually good penetrators but do not expand once in the target. They are often referred to as "ball ammo." Jacketed bullets are also "cleaner," leaving fewer metal deposits in the barrel. FMJ cartridges are inexpensive and thus usually what you'll buy to practice with at the range.

A jacketed hollow point (JHP) contains an opening at the tip of the jacketed bullet. This opening causes the bullet to expand upon hitting a target, dumping all the energy of the bullet into the target and causing a significant wound. This is why JHP are most often used as defensive ammunition against two-legged assailants.

Jacketed Hollow Point cartridge

Some hollow points are filled with a small rubber insert, or polymer plug. The plug enhances the JHP's penetrative ballistics. For example, when a regular hollow point penetrates an attacker, the hollow point can become clogged with bits of clothing and other materials such as bone or tissue. This slows the bullet down and can decrease both penetration and expansion. The silicone plug allows the bullet to fully penetrate and still expand for terminal ballistic performance. Additionally, while less a factor at self defense distances, the hollow point plug enhances bullet aerodynamic properties, reducing the drag caused by air rushing into the bullet tip.

Polymer insert in a jacketed hollow point

Contrasted with FMJ, hollow points are less effective at penetration. But whereas ball ammo may produce a "through and through" wound on an attacker, with little internal, stop-the-threat damage (unless it hits a vital organ or spine/central nervous system), a hollow point will expand in the body, causing all sorts of damage, including tissue hemorrhaging and *hydrostatic shock*.

Hydrostatic shock is caused by the kinetic energy of the projectile and the ballistic pressure shock wave it produces within the fluid-filled soft tissues of a body. This type of physical shock can disrupt the physiological function of other tissues and organs not directly impacted by the initial wound. Hydrostatic shock can in some cases incapacitate (stop the threat of) the recipient of a bullet wound faster than blood loss. Neurological disruption or impairment can result from a projectile impact that doesn't hit the brain or central nervous system, due to the effects of hydrostatic shock.

Discussions about cartridges, ammunition, hydrostatic shock, etc… invariably lead back to a discussion of the *best* caliber. Ultimately, it comes down to simple physics. Caliber discussions involve myriad variables-too many of which to go into in a book like this. Examples of the broad spectrum of considerations regarding which caliber is best for self defense include length of barrel, size and weight of the bullet, velocity of the bullet, revolver vs. semi auto, amount of clothing on a "bad guy" (penetration requirement to get through to vitals), JHP vs. FMJ, size of wound hole/channel, whether or not the target person is impaired by drugs, etc… and the list goes on and on. But again, ultimately it comes down to shot placement.

The one caveat that does prioritize caliber "size" almost as importantly as shot placement is if you are using your firearm for defense against four-legged predators. In most cases, we'd recommend a separate gun for hiking in the wilderness where you might encounter a large animal like a bear. For such a scenario, a "bigger" caliber is almost always better. So for example, if your daily carry gun is a 9mm, you'd be much better served against large North America predators with a .357, 10mm, or anything that starts with a "4" (i.e. .41 Magnum, .44 Magnum, .454 Casull…). But since this book is primarily about choosing a firearm for defending against two-legged threats, we make this passing reference to larger calibers being more suitable for defense against larger predators.

Choosing a defensive caliber is much simpler than the endless "caliber wars" would indicate, and doesn't require a doctorate in physics. The most important emphasis, oft repeated here, should always be on shot placement rather than caliber. A well-placed shot from a .22 caliber is almost always more effective at *stopping the threat* than a haphazardly or inaccurately fired round from a "man-stopper" like the .357. That said, it stands to reason then that an accurately placed shot from a .357 will almost always settle the matter in your favor. So your *frequency and consistency of practice* should be your focus, more so than which caliber you choose.

CHAPTER 6

HOME DEFENSE FIREARMS-SHOTGUNS

The intent of this book is to provide you with helpful information on choosing a gun or guns for every day carry (EDC) and self defense. While a gun chosen for EDC self defense will also serve well as gun for defense of your home, there are other options that are potentially better when the parameters required for a "carry" gun are removed.

However, just because you are at home doesn't mean you must take off your everyday carry gun; there's no reason you can't continue to wear your firearm just because you are in your house. What could be a better home defense gun than the one never more than 12 inches from your hand at any moment? Even if you don't wear it, you can have it close at hand, on the counter, shelf, or nightstand. *If you have kids or guests in your home you are still responsible to make sure your firearm is safely secured, out of reach, or out of sight.* This is much easier to do if you are wearing it and in complete control of it.

There are too many tragic stories of gun-owning homeowners maimed or murdered by intruders; when the police investigated the crime scene, they found that the house was full of defensive firearms.

The homeowner was caught by surprise and sadly never had time to make it to the closet or safe where the guns were stored.

Wearing your firearm in your home doesn't make you paranoid-it makes you prepared. It's a good habit too because the more you wear your holstered firearm- especially when you are just starting out with everyday carry- the faster it will feel normal. Carrying will become more comfortable, and comforting. Plus, if you have children living in the house, you will always know where your gun is and that it is secure.

Before we go on, there are two crucial and often insufficiently considered aspects of which to be aware when incorporating a firearm in your home defense plan. The first is **over-penetration** of your fired bullet- through walls, doors, and into rooms occupied by loved ones. Over penetration can largely be controlled by selecting the right ammo for handguns, shotguns, and rifles. Just as hollow points are some of the best options for your every day carry handgun, they will also usually be effective indoors. On the other hand, full metal jacket ammo will likely penetrate through drywall and hollow doors, potentially perilously in the direction of family members on the other side.

The second factor to consider when planning a firearm home defense plan is noise *decibel level*. The report (sound) coming from a fired gun of any type is **LOUD**, which is why we wear hearing protection at the range. In a self defense situation, you are unlikely to be wearing any type of hearing protection; thus potential hearing damage (short term or possibly permanent) is the price you pay for protecting your life and the lives of your loved ones. Inside a house, the decibel level of a fired weapon can be painful to unprotected ears. Granted, your survival is more important than any adverse affect on your hearing, but you should be aware of the noise and how it affects everyone in your family, especially young children and their sensitive eardrums.

Bottom line, hearing health is secondary to your *survival*. Short of buying a *suppressor* (not a silencer) the loud *bang* of a gun fired in self defense is just a reality- nothing to be feared- but it's worth mentioning.

Just as in choosing a handgun for every day carry, the same rules apply in choosing a home defense firearm-you'll want ease of operation and unquestioned reliability. The best alternatives to handguns for home defense are **long guns**-*shotguns* and *carbines*. Long guns are favored for their accuracy and power. An empty long gun can also be used as a blunt force battering weapon if need be.

Thunder Ranch Firearms president Clint Smith is a firearms expert; he's a retired Marine who served in Vietnam, a former SWAT team leader, and is a weapons and tactics instructor. He tells the following anecdote:

"*The old sheriff was attending an awards dinner when a lady commented on his wearing his sidearm. "Sheriff, I see you have your pistol. Are you expecting trouble?"' The sheriff said, 'No ma'am. If I were expecting trouble, I would have brought my rifle."*

While nobody wants to live their life "expecting" trouble, there's no reason one can't prepare for it before it shows up at the front door. If trouble does show up at your door, a shotgun or rifle provides the most threat-stopping power you can bring to bear. Smith states that in any violent encounter "*The handgun would not be my choice of weapon if I knew I was going to a fight. I'd choose a rifle, a shotgun…*"

Your daily carry gun should be the best gun for you in preparation for whatever self defense scenario you're likely to encounter outside the home. In defending the more static environment of your home and family members therein, you can plan a bit more specifically and deliberately. You know the layout of your house; where the entry and exits are, the bedrooms, the bathrooms, windows, crawl spaces, doors to the attic and the basement. The same is true if you live in an apartment. With practical preparation, you can plan and anticipate the best way to keep you and your family safe.

A long gun is going to offer you the best potential for accuracy, versatility and power. One of the best choices for the purpose of defending your home is the ***pump action shotgun***, followed closely by a ***semi-auto shotgun***. There are other shotguns, like the double barrel, side by side and over under models- all of which are effective (and fun!), but modern high quality **h**ome **d**efense (**HD**) shotguns are single barrel, multiple rounds (shells) pump or autoloaders. *The power and effectiveness of a single shell from a shotgun at close range is unrivaled.*

Remington 870 with 18-inch barrel

Operationally, a pump shotgun is like a combination of a revolver and a semi-auto handgun. It possesses revolver simplicity and reliable functionality, but it does require manual operation to *cycle and chamber* a round, similar to the pulling of the slide on a semi auto handgun. A pump shotgun will work under just about any condition, clean or dirty, with cheap ammo as well as more expensive high power, low recoil ammo. You could go into grandpa's closet and find a pump shotgun that's stood untouched, covered in dust for the last 40 years, load it, chamber a round, and barring any mechanical issue, it will assuredly fire.

It's a misconception that you don't need to carefully *aim* a shotgun, assuming that the spray *pattern* will simply hit whatever is in the general direction the barrel is pointed. Compared to a handgun or rifle round, you do have a moderately wider margin of error given that shotgun rounds, particularly those for home defense, do *spread out,* whereas a single round from a handgun or rifle will not. However, *margin of error* in the case of a home defense shooting could mean the difference of hitting your target (bad guy) or the *error* of also hitting a family member in front, to the side, or behind the target (bad guy)- so aiming a shotgun is still *fundamentally necessary*. The *spray pattern* of shotgun pellets or *shot* is dependent upon the distance to the target; the pattern *grouping* decreases the closer the distance.

Diagram of a pump action shotgun
Mossberg 930 SPX 8-shot autoloader 18.5" barrel
Image courtesy of Mossberg

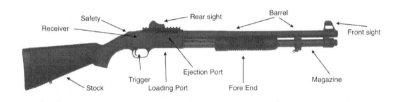

The pump action shotgun includes a sliding action *forend* grip that is "pumped" (pulled toward you and then pushed forward) to cycle a round into the chamber. Stock pump actions are typically 3-5 rounds, but with *magazine tube extensions* can have up to 10 rounds. For home defense (**HD**), the ideal length of the barrel is 18-20 inches. Short enough to maneuver comfortably in the house and around corners, an HD shotgun will generally be capable of holding 5-8 rounds. This is not to say that a 26 inch hunting shotgun isn't adequate for home defense, because it is. But longer barrel shotguns do come with a weight and maneuverability disadvantage inside the confines of a house.

Semi-auto or *autoloading* shotgun operates differently than a pump action; once a semi-auto magazine tube is loaded, a round is chambered by the single pulling back and release of the *charging handle.* Whereas a pump action shotgun requires the manual "pumping" of the gun for each round, a semi-auto shotgun will continue to shoot with each pull of the trigger until the last shell is fired. *Most* semi-auto shotguns are called "recoil loaders" because it is the gas-powered recoil operation (blowback) that cycles the next round (similar to a semi-auto handgun).

Autoloading shotgun
FN SLP 12 gauge 18-inch barrel
Image courtesy of FN America

Semi-auto shotguns require more maintenance than pump actions. They tend to get dirtier faster due to the gas blowback operation. They are also often *ammo sensitive-* whereas a pump action will shoot everything from cheap chain store ammo to high quality low recoil shells, semi-autos may not, or at least not reliably and consistently enough to offer a home defense advantage over a pump action. Semi-autos are not a bad options if that's what you've got, but in discussing home defense options the pump action is arguably a better first choice option.

Shotgun cartridges

Shotgun cartridges are called **shells**. Shotgun caliber is measured as *gauge*. The gauge (**ga.**) of a shotgun is the measurement of the gun's barrel bore diameter. The larger the bore diameter, the larger the projectile or projectiles that are capable of propelling from the bore; the larger the projectile(s), the more threat-stopping damage can be done to the target.

The two most common gauges for home defense shotguns are 12 and 20 gauge. 12 and 20 gauge are also popular for hunting so depending upon the length of barrel, your HD shotgun can also double as a hunting shotgun *if necessary*. However, we recommend a separate shotgun dedicated to each primary task for which it is intended (with the added bonus is that it may still be capable of a secondary task). Your life *demands* this consideration.

Shotgun shells are similar to handgun and rifle cartridges in terms of internal construction. The primer is located in the base of the brass head. The primer sparks and ignites the gunpowder charge, which propels the **wad** and the **shot**. The wad is typically a plastic piece that separates the shot from the powder charge. The *shot* are the actual projectiles, or pellets, varying in size and number depending upon the application for which they are intended.

Shotgun cartridge diagram
Courtesy of the NRA

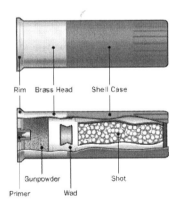

There are three main categories of shotgun shells. **Birdshot** is typically used for hunting fowl and is composed of the *smallest size and highest number of pellets*. Traditionally made of lead but now mostly of steel, birdshot has a generally wider spread pattern to hit birds "on the wing," or flying in the air. Fowl is most often a moving target, in the air, at distances greater than what would be considered self defense range.

Buckshot is smaller in number but larger in size than birdshot. Buckshot gets its name because the load was historically used to kill game as large as "buck deer." It is the law enforcement short range standard for duty shotguns. Buckshot loads are what you'll likely want for your HD shotgun because it is ferociously effective, hurling multiple solid spherical balls at short range within a relatively small grouping on target. "Double-ought" (00) buck puts approximately 8 projectiles totaling 3/4-1/2 oz. in weight on target. Buckshot can penetrate drywall and other home surfaces, so it is crucial one be aware what and who is *behind* the intended target.

Slugs are a solid piece of lead or steel and are often the most lethal of accurately fired shotgun projectiles. Like a handgun or rifle bullet, a slug is a single projectile, but in contrast to a single round from a handgun or rifle, a slug is much larger and heavier. Compared to handgun or rifle bullets, a shotgun slug is the equivalent of a cannon ball.

Slugs are more accurate and travel at a higher velocity than birdshot or buckshot; they are generally too fast and too powerful to use for home defense because they will pass right through the bad guy and then through the wall behind him into the next room. There's no spread pattern with a slug like there is with birdshot and buckshot. Slugs are often used for hunting big game or extreme penetration of things like vehicles and other barriers. If you're defending a big home or ranch, a slug might be appropriate, but for apartments and most other homes, you are better off with buck or bird shot.

When using a shotgun for home defense, the most important requirement is still shot placement. As with handguns, shotgun recoil (usually determined by the gauge) is a major factor contributing to accuracy. Shotguns are known for "big" recoil, although the recoil can be mitigated by low-recoil rounds that still provide all the necessary power and spread pattern.

The lower the number of the gauge, the bigger the bore; the bigger the bore, the bigger the felt recoil. For example, you'll experience less felt recoil with a 20 gauge than with a 12 gauge shotgun. So if you choose a shotgun for home defense, you need to know the threshold with which you are personally comfortable. It's a good idea to shoot a few different shotguns and gauges before you decide.

You also need to know the capabilities of your family members living in the house with you. In a multiple threat home invasion, one of your family members may need to operate your shotgun while you operate your handgun or other rifle (to be discussed shortly). So even if you can operate a 12 gauge shotgun with ease, your spouse, son or daughter may only be able to effectively handle a 20 ga. How do you determine these thresholds? Trial, practice, and more practice.

Why do we advocate a pump action shotgun more than a semi automatic for home defense? Wouldn't a single charge of a semi-auto, followed by the ease of pulling the trigger as many times as needed make it a better choice? Perhaps for some people with prohibitive physical conditions, that may well be true.

Overall however, a pump shotgun is about as straightforward as it gets. One pump, one round. Not only is it a simple manual process of which most people are capable, but the pump action is also an inherent safety feature. Even if the safety on the pump action isn't engaged (both pump actions and autoloaders typically have safeties), the gun will only fire if a round if chambered, and the only way to chamber a round is to pump the shotgun. In a high stress situation, manually pumping the gun may keep you from accidentally firing more rounds than necessary.

People often discuss the psychological impact the sound a pump action makes. Most sane people hear the definitive "chuk chuk" that signifies potential and impending pain or death by multiple lead balls and they stop whatever nefarious action they are doing or plan to do. The problem is, most criminals invading your home aren't considered sane, and they may not value their lives as much as they value ruining yours and stealing what isn't theirs.

So if you pump your shotgun to "scare" or warn the bad guy, you also signal where you are in your house, thereby losing your element of surprise and tactical advantage. There's no such thing as a fair fight when you are defending yourself, your loved ones or your home. As Jeff Cooper said, "*if you find yourself in a fair fight, your tactics suck.*"

Remember, you should never use your self defense firearm specifically to *warn an attacker*; use your powerful voice whenever *reasonably* necessary or possible. If you draw your gun in a defensive situation, *you must have the intent to use it to* **stop the threat**, however necessary.

CHAPTER 7

HOME DEFENSE: CARBINES

Most people are familiar with the modern version of the ubiquitous black rifle, the AR-15. The AR's *fully automatic* relative, the M-16, has been in the living rooms of Americans since its service during the first "television" war in Vietnam. Hollywood, the mainstream media and gun-grabbing politicians have unfairly dubbed the "AR" platform as a "military weapon," "assault rifle," and "evil black gun" and have pushed the narrative that it is a "machine gun" worthy of our fear and ire.

In reality the AR platform is a simple, reliable **semi-automatic** rifle with a typical magazine capacity of 30 rounds. In states where stock high capacity magazines are disallowed, 10-round magazines are standard. The AR is increasingly viewed and used as a viable option for home defense. A handgun or shotgun for self defense is a blunt force tool; an AR-15 at close range is a precision instrument capable of extraordinary threat-stopping power.

Windham Weaponry MPC AR-15 with iron sights and carry handle
Image courtesy of Windham Weaponry

Contrary to pervasive myth, "**AR**" *does not* stand for *Assault Rifle*. The original design of the AR-15 was invented and manufactured by the firearm manufacturing company **ArmaLite**. In designating all of their rifles, ArmaLite used the first two letters of their company name -AR- followed by a model number. Prior to the creation of the AR-15, ArmaLite manufactured the AR-1, AR-5, AR-7, and AR-10.

In 1956, US Army officials asked ArmaLite to produce a smaller version of the company's AR-10 (7.62x51mm) as a successor to the legendary WWII and Korean War fighting rifle, the M1 Garand. Thus, the 5.56x45mm caliber **AR-15** was born.

In 1959, ArmaLite licensed the AR-10 and AR-15 to **Colt's Manufacturing Company**. This lead to the AR-15 platform eventually becoming the military model M-16. As the AR designation has become synonymous with the rifle platform itself, numerous companies today produce semi automatic AR-type rifles in various calibers. This co-opted model classification as a *type* of rifle is cause for some confusion. However, there is no confusion as to the efficacy and potency of a semi automatic AR rifle.

Rifles with barrels shorter than 18 inches are often called carbines. The famous M4 carbine is the shorter and lighter version of the M16. Think of it this way; all carbines are rifles, but not all rifles are considered carbines. So technically, your AR-15 might be considered a carbine rather than a rifle, but the terms carbine and rifle are often used interchangeably.

In considering the AR as a home defense firearm, we'll discuss the AR-15 chambered in **5.56x45mm NATO/.223 Remington**. The standard AR for home defense has a 16-16.5 inch length barrel.

The AR is as reliable as it is simple. A semi automatic AR is comprised of 4 main components- a *lower receiver, upper receiver, stock, and a barrel.*

4-part Anatomy of an AR-15

The **lower receiver** (often just called a lower) includes the trigger and hammer assemblies, pistol grip, fire/safety switch, magazine well and magazine release button. The lower (including the external magazine) houses and transfers the cartridge from the magazine to the upper.

The **upper receiver** (upper) houses the bolt, bolt carrier, forward assist, charging handle, firing pin, and factory sights (if applicable). The upper receives the cartridge from the lower, and is where the round is *chambered*.

The **stock** rests against the shooter's shoulder, for stability and recoil absorption. In most modern ARs the stock is adjustable in length for the comfort of the individual shooter.

Finally, the **barrel** is the part of the rifle through which the bullet travels toward the target.

AR-15 rifle barrels are generally chrome lined (for corrosion and wear resistance) and "rifled" inside; **rifling** are the internal spiraling *lands* and *grooves* that impart spin on the bullet as it travels through the inside of the barrel. Measured in *twist rates*, the rifling adds to the bullet's aerodynamic *stability*, *velocity*, and *accuracy*.

Rifling, including lands and grooves
Image courtesy of the NRA

Twist rates in AR-15s are typically measured as ratios, i.e. 1:9. This means that the bullet will twist (rotate completely) once in as many inches designated; in a 1:9 twist barrel, the bullet will rotate completely once every 9 inches of barrel length. Defensive ARs typically have twist rates of **1:7, 1:8, 1:9**. A general rule of thumb- the lower the second number in the ratio, the faster the twist.

Twist rate and bullet stabilization

Image courtesy of the NRA

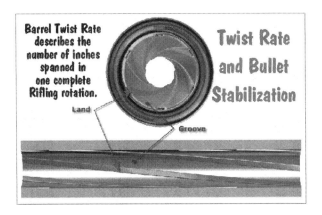

How does twist rate affect the bullet? A ratio such as a 1:7 means that the barrel can effectively stabilize a heavier 77 or 80 grain bullet (.223/5.56). A higher ratio like 1:9 is effective for stabilizing an average 50-62 gr. bullet. Most defensive .223/5.56 cartridge bullets are in the 50-62 gr. range, so the next consideration is the range within which you intend to shoot.

If you buy a rifle for home defense to be used at typical distances out to 50 yards, *any* of the twist rates between 1:7 to 1:9 will suffice. AR cartridges are tremendously powerful and accurate so you needn't be concerned with bullet stability or accuracy at short ranges (closer than 100 yards).

If you want to shoot heavier bullets at longer ranges (beyond 300 yards) you may consider a barrel with a 1:7 or 1:8 twist. Longer distances are more likely in hunting or recreational target shooting, which may cause you to consider a different caliber and rifle altogether. *Remember your primary reasons for buying a gun and purchase accordingly.*

The 5.56 NATO and .223 Remington cartridges are essentially identical in dimension, so why the two cartridge specifications?

Technically, the 5.56 is a NATO-spec (military) designation while .223 is the civilian (non-military) version. The simple explanation is that the cartridges can be loaded to different pressures and have a slightly different chamber *throat*. If your barrel is stamped .223 only, the higher pressures of 5.56 ammunition may not allow the casing to expand as it should during firing. However, a 5.56 barrel will accomodate both .223 and 5.56. Bottom line- both .223 and 5.56 are *more than sufficient* for home defense. Just make sure you know what your AR barrel is designed to handle. The *Wylde* barrel (created by Bill Wylde) is capable of handling both .223 and 5.56 equally well.

Considering its war fighting pedigree, one might assume the AR-15 rifle is "too much gun" for home defense use. Any firearm is be too much gun if the shooter isn't versed its capabilities. The AR-15 is indeed a high power, accurate, multiple round defense tool, and is an extremely effective tool in the hands of a practiced shooter.

Compared to shotguns, AR-15s are typically lighter and more maneuverable, have a higher capacity, exhibit much less recoil and are easy for just about everyone in the family to shoot. Carbines enjoy the same advantages over handguns, aside from the size and weight. Another advantage of the carbine is its superior accuracy; at short distances the rifle allows for near pinpoint shot placement. The low recoil allows for equally accurate follow up shots as necessary.

As you've learned about handgun and shotgun ammunition, the threat-stopping power of a rifle is largely contingent on cartridge selection. Therefore, what's the best .223/5.56 for self defense in the home? You guessed it-a hollow point. Why? Remember, hollow points allow for more transfer of energy *into* the target, rather than *through* the target. Any of the solid "ball" ammo cartridges travel too fast and don't expand, which means they will zip right through the bad guy (and through a wall or door behind him). If you miss a vital organ or central nervous system pathway, you might not stop your threat immediately. You want expansion, transfer of energy, and hydrostatic shock to end the malfeasance of the intruder. Even though the velocity of most .223/5.56 can still cause through and through soft tissue wound channels, hollow points give you the best chance at delivering threat-stopping shots on target. Plus, hollow points are more likely to slow down and break apart when they encounter solid (non-targeted) objects like doors, walls, and furniture.

Hornady VMAX hollow point bullet (note expansion "mushroom")
Image courtesy of Hornady Manufacturing

Another huge advantage of the AR-15 for defense is the low cost of the ammo. Both range practice and defensive cartridges are relatively inexpensive. Since cost can be a factor in how often you can afford to practice, low cost ammunition is a real bonus. With the firepower of an AR-15 you want to practice as often as possible, especially as a beginning shooter.

Most of the readily available .223/5.56 defensive ammo is 50-62 gr. You can't go wrong with the top brands, some of which are Hornady,

Winchester, Remington, Sig Sauer, Barnes, and CorBon. Look for ammo marked for self defense, claiming good expansion.

For practice ammo, anything your local range, Walmart or sporting goods store sells for will be sufficient. Practice ammunition will likely be full metal jacket ball ammo and there's no noticeable difference in the operation or performance of your rifle while shooting hollow points vs. ball ammo.

Remember what we discussed about "tacticool" modifications? The AR aftermarket is *filled* with them, and many enthusiast shooters decorate their AR like a Christmas tree. People often add sights, optics, new triggers, forward pistol grips, lights, bayonets, new "furniture" (AR-speak for different stocks, grips and forends) and the list goes on.

It can be fun and tempting to customize your AR. In our opinion, it is still best to keep your defensive weapons as simple as possible-K.I.S.S. If an accessory add-on definitively improves the weapon's functionality, fit, or (personal to you) comfort- *and* it improves fast, accurate, safe shooting-go for it. But if it makes a fundamental change to the internal workings or maneuverability (including weight and balance), then we suggest you pass.

A simple AR is as we discussed above-4 main components, and often includes the rudimentary but *extremely effective* addition of iron sights-which are perfectly suitable out to 150 yards (well in excess of *normal* self defense range). If you buy your weapon for home defense, you're unlikely to claim self defense out that far! But you will be fast on the draw inside your house and around the perimeter.

Aftermarket sights or optics may benefit your ability to acquire your sight picture more *accurately* but not necessarily *faster*. Also, be aware that they typically require batteries (which can run out of juice at the most inconvenient time), and can break if you drop your carbine on a hard surface. So unless you have a visual impairment that necessitates the use of an optic, you don't *need* one for a home defense AR.

There are numerous high quality AR carbines/rifles manufacturers. Expect to pay around $600 for a reputable new AR, but you can pay into the thousands of dollars for a high end model. Are the expensive ARs that much better? They may have smoother triggers and actions, but for home defense ranges those benefits don't really matter. The bottom line is that you *can* spend more, but for a high quality, reliable AR you don't *need* to break the bank.

Look for offerings from Windham Weaponry, ArmaLite/Eagle Arms, Daniel Defense, Ruger, Rock River Arms, Smith & Wesson, Sig Sauer, Bushmaster, and Stag Arms.

What about other (non-AR) rifles and carbines? How about a lever action, or shorter bolt action rifles? The clear advantage of the AR platform is multiple round capability quickly, that doesn't require repeated manual lever or bolt operation between trigger pulls.

That said, there are other rifles and carbines not in the AR category that will definitely work as home defense firearms. In fact, as with any "best" discussion, the best home defense firearm is the one you have in hand when you need it. Once again it comes down to your ability to quickly put threat-stopping rounds on target. If you can quickly put your front sight on target, and accurately hit your target, most carbines or rifles can serve you well in a defensive scenario.

Some carbines fire pistol calibers; these can also be good for home defense because you can keep your defensive calibers consistent. 9mm handguns and 9mm carbines use the same ammo, just as a lever action .44 Magnum will use the same ammo as your .44 Magnum revolver. Rifles and carbines will simply enhance the ballistic performance of your handgun calibers, notably accuracy and velocity- and thus threat stopping capability.

We discuss the AR-15 at length here because it checks off *all* the boxes in terms of ease of use, reliability, simplicity, firepower, and threat-stopping accuracy. As a bonus, it also has fun and useful secondary applications!

CHAPTER 8

HOLSTERS AND OTHER METHODS OF CARRY FOR HANDGUNS

Now that you've made the commitment to carry your handgun everyday, you also need a comfortable means to securely *retain* or conceal your new sidearm. It's called a sidearm for a reason, as it should always be at your side, or at least close to you- quickly and easily accessible. The most common means to keep your firearm on or near your person are holsters and purses. Attachés and backpacks are also considerations, and they will be covered in the discussion of handbags.

Open vs. Concealed Carry

Open carry simply means your handgun will be worn visibly, outside your clothing. The number of states that allow open carry without a permit varies from year to year so check your local and state laws. Visit www.handgunlaw.us- it's a great online resource to stay current on state-by-state gun laws.

Concealed carry means that your firearm will be concealed on your person, under clothing, and not openly visible. Carrying a firearm concealed requires a permit in most states, but an increasing number of states allow for *Constitutional or* permitless carry, open or concealed. We think this is a great thing and is provided for by the 2nd Amendment, though we still encourage gun owners to take the extra step to obtain a permit.

Carry permits vary by state, but you'll find it identified as a Concealed Handgun License/Permit (**CHL/CHP**), Concealed Carry Weapons (**CCW**) permit, Concealed (Defensive/Deadly) Weapon Permit/License (**CDWL/CWP/CWL**), Concealed Carry Permit/License (**CCP/CCL**), License To Carry (Firearms) (**LTC/LTCF**), Carry of Concealed Deadly Weapon license (**CCDW**), and a Concealed Pistol License (**CPL**).

If the option is available to you, we *highly recommend* that you acquire your concealed carry permit. While not always obligatory, it is a good step that provides further validation that you are a responsible gun owner. Obtaining a permit to carry requires a few hours of classwork, with the additional benefit to you of learning your local and state gun laws. A carry permit gives you the utmost in flexibility to choose how you want to carry your firearm-concealed or open. Permits typically allow state to state reciprocity-the legal ability to carry in a state in which you do not reside.

There are a variety of different holster styles and means to attach or keep your firearm close to your body. The two most common are Inside the Waist Band (**IWB**) and Outside the Waist Band (**OWB**). Both allow for open carry and concealed carry but vary in terms of *concealability*. There are also *shoulder holsters, chest holsters, and ankle holsters.*

IWB/OWB are the most prevalent holsters worn on your waist. If you choose to wear a belt holster, you must also have a belt specifically made for holding a weapon in a holster. The belt can be leather or made of other material, as long as it is thick and supportive enough to carry the weight of your firearm. Some gun belts are even steel lined.

Regular belts will not do the job for anything bigger than the smallest and lightweight firearms.

OWB holster

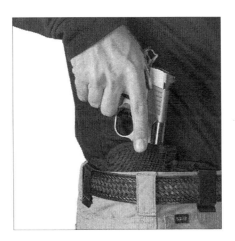

IWB holster
Courtesy of the NRA

A variation of an OWB holster is a **paddle**. Paddle holsters don't require your holster to go through a belt loop, and can be worn IWB or OWB. Paddles are often used if you have to take your holster off frequently, i.e. going in and out of federal or government buildings, schools etc...

Paddle Holster

Shoulder holsters can be a good alternative to waist-worn holsters as they distribute the weight of the firearm under your non-shooting shoulder. A shoulder worn firearm is typically accessed by reaching across your body.

Shoulder Holster
Courtesy NRA

While comfort is a positive benefit of shoulder holsters, you lose some speed in drawing your firearm, especially if you are wearing it under clothing or a jacket. Upon drawing cross-body from a shoulder holster position, your firearm will most likely face backward and angled down, necessitating that you "sweep" multiple planes with your barrel upon drawing, possibly putting a lot of innocent targets at risk in a tense self defense scenario. However, training with your shoulder holster can help mitigate these potential drawbacks.

Chest holsters are similar to shoulder holsters, offering a secure fit to the body. Chest "rigs" are most often used to carry larger caliber, heavier handguns that would be uncomfortable to wear on the hip. Many wilderness guides and outdoorsman carry their large caliber handgun in a chest rig worn outside their clothing for quick and unimpeded access to defend against attacks from large animals like grizzlies.

Chest holster

Ankle holsters offer great concealment when worn securely under a pant leg. Given the space and location, ankle holsters are typically used to hold compact firearms, sometimes a primary firearm or more typically a back up. Ankle holsters provide an option for the ease and flexibility of carrying two guns; including one worn by the other retention methods discussed above. An ankle holster is often worn on the inside of your off hand (non-shooting hand) leg, for ease of "cross-leg" draw. Wearing an ankle holster takes a little getting used to, and you'll want to make sure your pant legs are loose enough to easily access your weapon if needed. Finally-a practical benefit of bell bottoms!

In addition to a holster or carry system for your handgun, we think it is equally wise to consider carrying a spare magazine holster. Just because you are armed and carrying doesn't mean you are as prepared as you can be. In today's society it is wise to carry a spare, fully loaded magazine with you. Overkill? We sure hope so, but nobody has ever been in a self defense situation and complained they had too much ammunition. Just because you have extra ammo doesn't mean you need to use it.

There are plenty of options for magazine holsters, including OWB mag holders worn on your belt. Of course, you can always carry a magazine in your pocket, but we advocate other more secure methods-you don't want your ammunition getting dirty with pocket lint, or getting tangled with keys or a cell phone in an emergency. You can also carry spare magazines in a hip pack or backpack, but as with purses or any other off body method, allocate a pocket dedicated to hold your spare magazine.

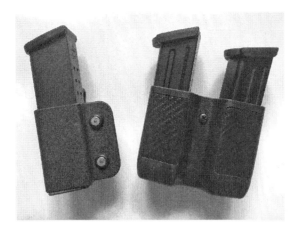

Single and double magazine holsters

If you carry a revolver, (and perhaps especially so given the capacity limits of a revolver cylinder) you should also carry additional ammo. How do you carry individual rounds? In a *speed loader*. This device holds the revolver ammo in place with a twisting mechanism; when you've loaded the rounds into the cylinder, you twist and release. There are speed loaders for each caliber as well as a variety of pouches to hold them. Some revolvers also allow for the use of *moon clips*, typically circular steel or plastic pieces that hold revolver cartridges together for fast loading and unloading as a single unit. (They are called "clips," as there is no feeding mechanism or spring).

Revolver Speed loaders

Holster materials

Holster materials traditionally include leather, Kydex (plastic), and ballistic nylon. The following is a brief description of the common materials and pros and cons. By no means an exhausting list, this will get you started as you determine which material in a holster works best for you.

Leather:

Pros: traditional, comfortable, durable, classy. Smooth leather is soft on the finish of the gun and leather holsters can look better with age if treated properly. Cons: sometimes leather can "sweat," causing condensation and potentially corrosion on the gun if not wiped down. Thick holsters, while durable, can be heavy and expensive.

Leather holster with standard and cross draw capability
Simply Rugged Holsters with basketweave design

Kydex:

Pros: durable, lightweight, typically molded to the specific gun model, can be inexpensive, waterproof and less susceptible to sweat. Cons: can be noisy upon drawing or reholstering; can also mar the finish on the guns. Depending upon thickness, Kydex can be rigid.

Kydex holster

Garrett Industries, Kydex molded over leather

Ballistic nylon:

Pros: lightweight, inexpensive, flexible, sometimes, but not always customized to fit a specific gun model or brand, versatile. Cons: over time, can become too flexible, retention is not always the most secure.

Ballistic nylon holster

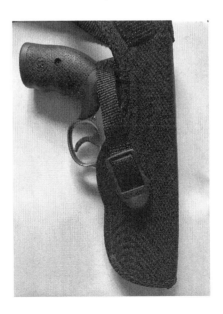

Some holster manufacturers like Garrett Industries in Woodville, Texas make holsters with Kydex molded to leather. The outside of the holster is durable, molded and customized Kydex. The inside of the holster is lined with leather which is soft on the gun and quiet on the draw.

Simply Rugged Holsters in Prescott, Arizona makes high quality leather holsters out of various types of leather, including alligator, cape buffalo and even shark skin!

Comfort, security, and safety should be your top criteria in the selection of a holster. If you are like most gun enthusiasts, you may have to try a handful of holsters to learn what is most comfortable and secure for you and the good news is there are a lot of options available. Just remember, you've made the investment in the firearm to protect yourself and loved ones; don't skimp on the choice and quality of a holster that you'll be wearing as often as you carry your gun. Think of a holster as an important accessory to your daily wardrobe.

Other methods of carry

For this section we'll focus primarily on purses, but we also recognize the need for men to sometimes carry off-body, so the principles discussed regarding a woman's purse will also apply to backpacks, brief cases, soft cover attachés, messenger bags, fanny or hip packs, etc… Of these methods, a fanny or hip pack provides the closest approximation to a holster (in terms of accessibility) and such packs are easily concealed under clothing or when worn outside clothing.

The single most important requirement for carrying a firearm in a purse, pack, bag, etc… is that your firearm be located in a *dedicated* pocket or slot. This is especially important in a woman's purse, where various items compete for space. Your weapon is your life defender, and it necessitates an easily accessed, secure location. If you must reach into your bag to quickly produce your firearm, you *must not* be forced to contend with keys, a cell phone, water bottle, billfolds, makeup, etc… You cannot afford to have anything get caught in the trigger either, which could cause a malfunction or worse-a *negligent discharge*[5] toward you, a family member, or other innocent bystanders.

Fortunately, there are companies producing fashionable gun-ready purses and handbags for women too. **Gun Tote'n Mamas** has a diverse selection of bags and totes, proving that women don't need to sacrifice style for security in deciding to carry a firearm. One of the advantages for women carrying a purse is that they don't have to limit themselves to a small snub nose handgun. There are many different sized purses, totes, and bags from which to choose to carry as large a caliber handgun as they desire.

Purse with dedicated firearm compartment

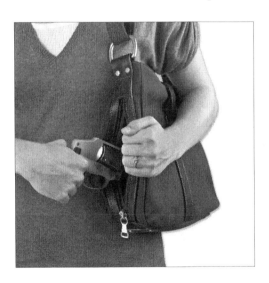

---

[5] Negligent discharge-accidental or unintentional firing of a round. This can happen in various ways, but usually occurs when the shooter unintentionally pulls the trigger without meaning to fire the gun.

Image courtesy of the National Rifle Association

Whichever method you choose for on-body or off-body carry of your EDC firearm, we encourage you to view a holster, purse, or bag as an accessory to your daily wardrobe. Whichever is most comfortable and convenient for you- ***just carry***. All the training, confidence, and competence with a self defense firearm means nothing if you don't have your gun with you when you need it. Wear it, get accustomed to it, and make it a part of your daily dressing routine. It will take some time to get use to it, but stick with it! Let your EDC become a mere extension of your ability and ***right*** to defend yourself.

CHAPTER 9

PHYSICAL CONSIDERATIONS AND RECOMMENDED EXERCISES

Regardless of an individual's physical size or strength, a firearm is a great equalizer in self defense. There are countless stories of single moms and elderly citizens defending themselves, their families, and their homes against bigger, younger, faster, marauding attackers. When you have a firearm with which you have practiced and become proficient, you are fully capable of defending yourself against most human or animal threats. Your newfound self-assurance alone is often your greatest asset, but it's nice to have your confidence bolstered by your firearm.

Men and women of all ages, ethnicities, and physical statures have made the brave decision to protect themselves with firearms. However, some people have physical conditions that must be considered in their selection of the appropriate firearm for their abilities. Smaller framed individuals, for example, may not be best served by choosing a large framed revolver or heavy full size 1911 semi auto. Hands are different sizes too. Some folks have conditions like arthritis or simply lack the requisite grip strength for bigger calibers and heavier guns. Some people have suffered strokes or endured surgery that prevents or inhibits the use of an arm or hand. Are these people be out of luck and at the mercy of criminals?

Absolutely not!

One must only be aware of any limiting factor and then work within those parameters to select the gun that allows them to shoot capably. Often, aside from a permanent injury or physical limitation, most "weaknesses" can be effectively addressed if not fully overcome.

Effective operation and shooting of a firearm does require varying degrees of strength, mainly in the hands. However, *never* let a lack of strength, real or perceived, stop you from getting a gun and practicing with it. Simply understand the main physical requirements to operate revolvers and semi autos, and make your firearm decision accordingly.

Hand and grip strength is required for both revolvers and semi autos- for racking the slide of a semi auto, and controlling recoil for follow up shooting in both revolvers and semis. You might need to clear a jam or resolve a failure to feed (FTF) in a semi, by gripping and pulling the slide back and releasing. Revolvers require 11-14 lbs. of trigger pull when shooting double action. Other than pulling the slide on a semi auto, shooting a revolver often requires more overall grip strength than the operation of a semi auto.

The actual physical grip of a handgun can be enhanced by a rubber grip or textured tape. Such aftermarket tape is often customized for a wide variety of guns and improves the grip of the shooter through a combination of texture and a millimeter or more of extra "padding." Talon Grips is a company that makes grip tape for a variety of handguns.

Textured grip tape

Image courtesy of Talon Grips

For revolvers, you can change out the stock grips with aftermarket hand grips to make the revolver feel smaller or larger in the hand. Many semi auto handguns today come with extra grip panels so you can add or subtract to the side panels or back strap. There are even slide-on grips which completely and securely cover the factory grips.

Grip panels

Image courtesy of Heckler and Koch

But wait- what about all we've repeatedly stated about not augmenting or "accessorizing" self defense firearms? Aftermarket additions or changes to the grip won't affect the *internal mechanical* operation or reliability of the gun- only your ability to properly hold the gun, to maximize your firm grip. Improving your grip is similar to choosing the right size shoes. If a grip accessory enhances the basic ergonomics and defensive shootability of your firearm, go for it.

Exercises

Even if you enhance the tactile grip of your firearm, it still won't address your overall grip strength. For that you need to "hit the gym" to gain *power* in your grip.

Hitting the gym doesn't necessarily mean you need to renew your gym membership and go pump iron. Even still, we do advocate overall health and fitness as a way to improve your shooting. Everything you do for the fitness and health of your body will definitively benefit your shooting. Exercise can improve your ability to move dynamically in a self defense situation while also helping control your heart rate both in practice and under stress. So if you want to start eating better, lift some weights, and participate in a cardiovascular regimen, we encourage it!

Grip strength

Grip strength is a fundamental pillar of good shooting. You can start by strengthening your hands and key parts of your arms, including your shoulders, since you typically hold the gun level to your eyes when you shoot). If your hand or grip weakness is correctable, you have tons of exercise options. Here are a few simple ones:

Squeeze a ball- it can be a tennis ball, racketball, rubber ball, etc… Talk about simple. Just squeeze repeatedly. Your hand and forearm will fatigue quickly, but if you keep at it, over time you will increase your strength and recovery. Squeezing a ball is a great stress reliever too!

Rubber rings- just as simple as squeezing a ball, rings have the benefit of varied tension. They come in different colors, each of which represents different "poundage" or squeeze weight, so you can start small and go up as your strength increases. Do a simple web search for "hand exercise rings."

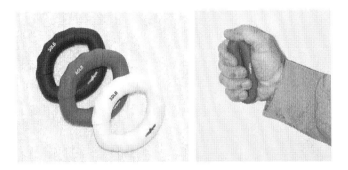

Rubber rings

Rice or sand- order up some rice, uncooked! Fill a bucket with uncooked rice or granular sand and dig your hands in. The resistance allows you to squeeze your hands together, rotate your wrists, extend your fingers, etc..., all of which help increase your grip strength and hand flexibility.

There are hundreds of different ways to improve your grip strength, many of which don't require specialized or expensive equipment. Resistance (or squeezing) exercises are generally the best because they help simulate the force you'll need to pull a trigger or stabilize recoil. Most of the resistance exercises allow you to work your fingers individually, which will really improve your overall hand strength.

Managing recoil is a key consideration as it relates to grip strength. Many new shooters think they are adversely "recoil sensitive" when shooting powerful calibers like .38 SPL, 9mm, and .357. Often, the truth is they just don't have the proper grip, or their grip strength is lacking. That's great news because this is most often corrected with a little strength training!

Don't ever let a lack of hand strength deter you from buying a gun and practicing with it. A firearm is an equalizer, an extension of your defensive mindset and physical ability to protect yourself!

CHAPTER 10

RECOMMENDATIONS

Our goal in sharing the information contained in this book is to help you find the right defensive firearm for you. We know that with the right selection of a revolver or semi-auto, shotgun or rifle, you will practice with it more, and in turn become more confident, comfortable and competent with your firearm. We desire to simplify your selection process by providing basic but often overlooked considerations.

Everyone has different requirements, capabilities, needs and desires and we're somewhat reluctant to promote any brand. However, many years of experience and traditional gun sales demonstrate that a few selections are qualified, "safe" choices. By safe we mean it's hard to go wrong with quality and reliability that millions have relied on for many years.

Further, after training hundreds of new shooters, we've come to appreciate that some firearms more than others consistently meet the criteria of *dependability, ease of use and maintenance*, and overall *quality and value*. Price is always a factor, so our suggestions focus on *value without compromise*. There are firearms in the each category for which you *can pay more, and they will often be equally good.* We simply point out that you don't *need* to pay more for a high quality, dependable firearm.

For defensive purposes, we remain focused on firearms in their stock configuration-this means no alterations to the original fire controls, no large sights or scopes, and no aftermarket magazine extensions. Further, we advocate factory ammunition (not handloaded) for both practice and defense.

Please see our short list of firearm models and brands we recommend unequivocally. Your choice in weight, size, and material construction depends on your personal capabilities, but the following brands and models are sound choices no matter what. Are there other good models, brands, and calibers? Certainly. But for personal self defense of you, your family, and your home, we think the following are excellent choices. We receive no compensation or consideration for these recommendations.

Handguns

Revolvers

Smith and Wesson snub 2" barrel in .38 Special (Spl)
Smith and Wesson 3-4" barrel in .38 Spl and .357
Ruger snub 2" barrel in .38 Spl
Ruger 3-4" barrel in .38 Spl and .357
Charter Arms 2" and 4" barrel in .38 Spl and .357

Semi-auto

Glock 9mm, .40 caliber, .45 caliber, 10mm (any "G" model)
Springfield Armory 9mm, .40 caliber
Heckler and Koch 9mm, .40 and .45 caliber (P30, HK .45, VP9)

FN 9mm (FNS 9)

1911 Semi auto

9mm and .45 options from **Springfield, Kimber, Colt, Wilson Combat, Ruger, Smith and Wesson**

Shotguns- *pump action*

Mossberg 500 and 590- 12 & 20 gauge
Remington 870- 12 gauge
FN P12- 12 gauge

AR-15 carbines

Windham Weaponry MPC
ArmaLite/Eagle Arms M15
Ruger AR-556

It's quite common for AR enthusiasts to build their own rifle by purchasing the components (upper, lower, trigger, etc…) separately. While this can sometimes be cost effective, we do not recommend it for your first AR. Buying a complete carbine or rifle from a reputable manufacturer has important advantages including tested, trusted dependability as well as a warranty. If anything goes wrong with the stock firearm, the company will stand behind their product. A mix and match build will not have the same guarantees.

Gun manufacturers have their production and quality control ups and downs, but the aforementioned companies have long track records of producing high quality, reliable firearms. There are other very good companies producing comparable quality firearms, but this list includes guns we use to protect ourselves and our families. We've personally shot, and/or owned, and vouch for each gun included on this list.

Your capabilities will determine what's right for you. Trial and research will lead you to the right gun as long as you stay focused on the basic requirements for a self defense firearm, whether a handgun, shotgun, or rifle.

CHAPTER 11

CASE STUDIES

Once someone has made the decision to purchase a gun for self or home defense, they too often go to their local gun store unprepared. By unprepared, we mean they haven't taken the appropriate steps that will help them determine what they need in a firearm.

It is not a lack of intelligence or sound intentions, but rather the fact that most new shooters simply don't know what questions to ask to educate themselves in the gun-buying process. After all, many people who make the decision to arm themselves wish they didn't need a gun in the first place, and they might not have previously given self defense or guns much thought.

In order to arm you with the information you need to make an educated decision on which firearm to purchase, we offer the following list of criteria to contemplate. Once you've identified these reasons for yourself, you'll be ready to wade through the sales advice you are likely to receive at the gun counter. Once you've got the gun "bug," you may want another gun for different application, so we've included criteria and factors beyond self defense.

For what application do you want a firearm?

Personal Defense/CCW/Daily Carry-handgun

Home Defense-handgun or long gun

Woods Defense handgun (hiking, camping, back up for hunting)

Competition/sport/target shooting-handgun or long gun

Once you've determined the application or intent for your purchase of a firearm, you should realistically rank for yourself the order of importance of the following factors. Since a home defense or outdoor protection firearm can be either a handgun or long gun (shotgun or rifle/carbine) we include such applications in the list of factors.

Firearm cost-how much are you willing to spend? Remember, more expensive does not always mean "better." But you do typically get what you pay for so don't go for a cheap firearm either.

Ammunition cost-some calibers are more expensive than others. This is an important consideration if you plan to shoot frequently.

Concealment-do you want a gun for discreet, concealed carry or will you carry openly (if your state laws allow)?

Ease of maintenance-are you willing to maintain the firearm diligently, or do you want a no fuss piece? This will in part be influenced by factors below.

Range of use-is this for short range (self defense) or long range (target) use? Remember, while some guns will fit a few categories, focus on what your primary intent or application (especially if it's for self defense).

Protection-is this for everyday carry personal protection, home defense, or outdoor/woods protection?

Operational simplicity-for handguns, are you willing and capable of operating the slide action of a semi automatic or do you prefer the pull-the-trigger straightforward action of a revolver? For long guns-can you pull the action of a pump shotgun or do you prefer the multiple round capability afforded by the single charge in a rifle or semi-auto shotgun?

Training commitment-this is one of the most important considerations, and one for which you owe yourself an honest answer. How much time are you willing to train and practice with your firearm? How many days per month will you commit to shooting? A highly committed shooter will go to the range 4 times per month or more. For many people, their honest answer is 4-6 times per year, or less. Perhaps you'll be somewhere in the middle, with more frequent practice in the early going.

Proficiency with a firearm is highly dependent on how much time one dedicates to training with it. Regardless of the firearm, the more one practices, the more proficient they will become. That said, some firearms do require more training to become competent in their use, i.e. a semi automatic with its slide action, and magazine loading. This is compared to a revolver that quite simply requires the shooter to point the gun and pull the trigger. Even still, consistently hitting the target with a revolver requires diligent training, especially when shooting a snub nose.

Once you've identified for yourself the application and intended use of your firearm and considered the key factors discussed above, you'll be well on your way to identifying which platform (revolver or semi auto) handgun you want, or which long gun (shotgun or carbine) best fits your personal needs. At a minimum, you'll be prepared to sift through the advice at your local gun store from your now more informed perspective. Just as you have taken it upon yourself to be your own first responder, you will be accountable for the decision you make on which gun to buy.

The following are real life examples of new gun buyers who consulted Bruce Owen on the purchase of their first gun. Each person came to

Bruce a novice, new to guns and shooting, but had determined they wanted a gun for self protection. Some were couples who made the decision together. After Bruce asked them the basic questions discussed above about their intended use and commitment level, he was able to make smart recommendations that would help the new shooters become proficient and self-reliant with their new firearms. Armed with such confidence, many quickly went on to buy additional firearms!

Case study #1

A single woman wanted a gun for personal protection, both inside and outside of the home. She was small in stature, and thus required a small, lightweight firearm to be concealed in her outerwear (jacket) or in a purse. She honestly determined that she would probably only practice 4-6 times per year, and thus wanted something simple, reliable, and easy to maintain. Recommendation? Revolver (Ruger LCR .38). The right questions led to the right firearm choice for this woman, who consistently hits center mass at 7 yards. She decided to take a CCW class from Bruce and is now a proud and confident CCW license holder!

Case study #2

A retired couple, both over the age of 65, wanted self defense firearms to carry in their car as they traveled between their summer and winter homes. Although they previously knew nothing about guns, a recent upsurge in crime in their home communities prompted this couple to get serious about their own self defense, while traveling and at home. They wanted a handgun and a long gun and they were committed to learning and training. Their one overriding request was that the firearms have an external safety mechanism.

After shooting a wide variety of handguns and rifles, they purchased the FNS9 (9mm) semi automatic handgun and Windham Weaponry AR-15

MPC (carbine). Both have shooting thumb-side external safety mechanisms, so although one is a handgun and the other is a rifle, the couple would be familiar with the general operation and safety features of both. Result? The couple is proficient not only in the firing of both weapons, but they can competently field strip and clean each firearm as well. They train twice a month and soon plan to add a shotgun primarily for home defense.

Case study #3

A young couple with very little firearm experience but a willingness to learn and train together wanted personal and home defense firearms. In their search for a handgun and long gun, they prioritized simplicity and reliability to protect their family. They handled and practiced with a variety of firearms. After assessing their strengths and capabilities, they purchased two Glock 43 (subcompact 9mm), a Remington 870 pump action shotgun, and an ArmaLite AR-15 carbine.

There are distinct benefits to the couple in having two of the same handgun; complete familiarity should they need to borrow the other person's handgun, in the same caliber with the same interchangeable magazines. The pump action shotgun was outfitted with a recoil absorbing butt pad, and loaded with low recoil buckshot and slugs. These additions do not affect the mechanics of the shotgun but allow it to be shot comfortably by the larger man *and* his smaller wife. The couple also easily learned to shoot and maintain the carbine. They store both of their long guns in a gun safe, easily accessible in their house. The husband and wife went on to receive their CCW licenses and now carry their G43s on their person at all times.

Case study #4

A middle aged woman who is an avid hiker wanted a firearm for self defense against 2-legged and 4-legged animals. She didn't hike in areas with large predators, so she didn't require big bore caliber protection. Although she was midsize in stature, the woman didn't mind carrying a slightly larger, heavier firearm. She was willing to invest the time to learn how to shoot her firearm safely and proficiently. She also committed to carrying her firearm, either in her purse or wearing it in an outside the waistband holster.

Bruce assessed that a midsize 9mm semi automatic was the right choice, and after shooting the Glock 19 and Springfield XDM, the woman found that while she was marginally more accurate with the Glock, she felt more confident with the XDM's passive grip safety and overall ergonomics. Her comfort and confidence level inspired her to train twice a month, which now also includes practicing with her new pump shotgun for home defense.

Case study #5

A retired military veteran who hadn't handled a firearm since his service in the Vietnam war decided it was time to purchase a handgun for his personal protection while driving and at home. Most of his military firearm experience was with rifles and 1911 style handguns, so he was eager to learn more about the "new" polymer striker fired semi automatic handguns. Although the basic design is more than 30 years old, he was keen to handle and shoot a Glock for the first time.

In short order, he learned how to accurately shoot a fourth generation full size Glock 17 in 9mm. He consistently hit center mass at 7 yards. Due to his dormant but not forgotten military training, as well as the simplicity of the Glock, he quickly learned how to disassemble the G17 for basic maintenance, as well as load, unload, and clear malfunctions. He now feels comfortable and secure in his travels and while at home.

Case study #6

This emotional example tells the story of an abused middle aged woman who had been savagely attacked with a knife, beaten and left for dead. Her attacker was captured and sent to prison. As his release date neared, the timid and solitary woman realized she needed to protect herself and concluded that a personal defense firearm was an important step toward her overall security. She suffered acute physical debilitation as a result of the years-ago attack but was not deterred in finding a firearm that would work for her.

While her overall arm strength was compromised, preventing consistent operation and disassembly of a semi-automatic, she did have sufficient hand and finger strength to operate a revolver. She was able to grip, shoot, and manage the recoil of a snub nose .38. Since she wanted to carry the weapon at all times, she selected a S&W lightweight in .38 SPL.

She obtained her CCW license and now carries her revolver every day. Her newfound confidence and self reliance inspired her to open up and develop relationships with her neighbors. The local police frequently drive by the woman's house, which she now shares with her new dog who dutifully barks at anyone passing by. Her firearm isn't her only form of self protection, but it is certainly an integral part of her overall self defense plan- and budding self assurance.

These case studies demonstrate that everyone is different in physical stature and capability and in their own personal needs and requirements in a firearm. Choosing a firearm shouldn't be a scary or difficult process. To make the right choice for you, it is important to do a little self evaluation of your needs and wants. After all, you're going to carry and train with this tool for your own self defense and perhaps that of your family. So a little pre-purchase thinking will go a long way toward selecting the best firearm for you.

CHAPTER 12

ADDITIONAL RESOURCES

There are a handful of national organizations dedicated to the defense of the 2nd Amendment and your right to bear arms. By sheer numbers, the **National Rifle Association (NRA)** and its **Institute for Legislative Action (ILA)** are the most prominent, and have the largest membership. The NRA is the strongest *political* gun rights lobby, and we encourage you to join. Visit www.nra.org.

There are many state level subsidiaries of the NRA/ILA, some more connected to the parent organization than others. Joining your state gun rights affiliate is a great way to stay on top of laws and legislators specific to your state. If every gun owner does this, it will strengthen the national level fight exponentially.

Gun Owners of America (GOA) is perhaps the most tenacious gun rights organization. Known as the *no-compromise gun rights lobby*, GOA is the Special Forces to the NRA's powerful conventional army. Join them both, as many do. Your money is well spent and in return for your membership contribution, you will receive all the support you need to launch your own individual advocacy efforts to force your state and federal legislators to comply with- and fight for- the 2nd Amendment. Visit www.gunowners.org.

The **Second Amendment Foundation (SAF)** is another tremendously worthy organization. SAF offers many educational and action-oriented resources in defense of the Constitution and our private right to bear arms. SAF is a complementary organization to the NRA and GOA. Visit www.saf.org.

Further reading:

Each of the aforementioned gun rights organizations offer and provide many helpful reading resources. Rather than listing key books here, we encourage you to visit the website of each organization to learn the books they offer. We strongly encourage you to start adding gun rights books to your reading list. Educate and arm yourself now with the tools for the ongoing legislative efforts.

Finally, one of the absolute best resources for information on current firearm law is www.handgunlaw.us. This outstanding online resource provides the most updated information on the laws in each state, reciprocity between states, and contains links to other valuable online gun-related websites. Handgun laws unfortunately change all too frequently so the responsible gun owner will stay on top of all such changes to continue to be a model law abiding gun owner. Please consider donating to www.handgunlaw.us!

Insurance:

You carry alls sorts of insurance-health insurance, car insurance, life insurance, homeowners insurance, etc… However none of these cover you in the event of a firearm related incident in which your life, family, and liberty is affected. Such an incident can be scary, litigious, and extremely expensive. We suggest you do some research into **Personal**

Firearm Liability insurance. The following are some of the most reputable vendors of such insurance.

Armed Citizens Legal Defense Network (ACLDN)- www.armedcitizensnetwork.org

CCWSafe- www.ccwsafe.com

US Concealed Carry Association- www.usconcealedcarry.com

Texas Law Shield- www.texaslawshield.com

US Law Shield- www.uslawshield

Second Call Defense- www.secondcalldefense.org

NRA Carry Guard- www.nracarryguard.com

Your right to self defense is both divinely provided and constitutionally protected. It is strange that we must fight to protect and defend this right, but such is the political climate today. In a perfect world, possessing guns for self defense wouldn't be necessary, but we don't live in a perfect world. Arming yourself isn't enough; now you must also join the millions of Americans who stand up for our individual and collective right to bear arms.

Thank you for your commitment to the defense of the Second Amendment.

Safety Rules

- Assume every firearm is loaded and handle it with utmost care
- Keep the barrel pointed in a safe direction until you are ready to fire at your target
- Do not aim at anything you do not intend to shoot or destroy
- Keep your finger off the trigger until you are ready to shoot
- Be sure of your target and what is behind your target
- Practice diligently with your firearm so you are prepared to use it in an emergency
- Perform basic cleaning and maintenance on your firearm to ensure its safe and reliable operation

ABOUT THE AUTHOR

Bruce Owen

Armed with more than 50 years of experience in the use and operation of firearms, Bruce Owen has a nearly encyclopedic knowledge of guns. He has trained more than 1000 "regular" citizens who now feel comfortable and confident in their ownership and use of firearms for self defense. Bruce has created simple training concepts to share his vast expertise in an informative and accessible manner with his students. His mission is to help his fellow American citizens achieve a high level of comfort and security with firearms. He created "Point of the Gun," a weekly podcast that evaluates new and used firearms. Bruce is an armorer for Glock and Smith & Wesson, is an NRA-certified firearms trainer and the founder of Survival Basics, a top notch concierge company specializing in survival gear. He lives in northern Arizona and offers his expertise to whomever wants to learn. Bruce can be reached at bruceowen@survivalbasics.net.

Doug Nickle

Doug Nickle is a political reformer and 2nd Amendment advocate. After graduating from the University of California, Berkeley, he played professional baseball, pitching in the Major Leagues for the Philadelphia Phillies and San Diego Padres. He is a dedicated proponent of citizen accountability and believes that only an engaged and informed electorate can effectively sustain the American Republic. A native of California, Doug lives with his wife, daughter, and four-legged children in the free state of Arizona.

Made in the USA
San Bernardino, CA
07 January 2018